Maunsell's Nelsons

Maunsell's Nelsons

D. W. Winkworth

London
GEORGE ALLEN & UNWIN
Boston   Sydney

First published in 1980

GEORGE ALLEN & UNWIN LTD
40 Museum Street, London WC1A 1LU

© D. W. Winkworth, 1980

British Library Cataloguing in Publication Data

Winkworth, Derek William
   Maunsell's Nelsons.
   1. Locomotives – England – History
   2. British Rail.   Southern Region – History
   I. Title
   385'.36'109422   TJ603.4.G   80-40160

ISBN 0-04-385079-0

Picture research by Mike Esau

Book designed by Diane Sawyer/Design Matters

Set in 11/12 Bembo by Inforum Ltd, Portsmouth
and printed in Great Britain
by Biddles Ltd, Guildford, Surrey

To the memory of
GFB

Contents

Illustrations

Tables

Preface

Mr Maunsell's largest locomotive design, the Lord Nelson, never gained the doubtful distinction of being a qualified success – let alone unqualified – before his successor had a look at the design. Perhaps the present examination of this small class might have been entitled *Maunsell's Enigma*: be that as it may, it must be admitted that the peculiar lack of general success that attended the class, coupled with a somewhat transitory mid-career improvement as a result of Mr Bulleid's modifications, had some attraction and prompted an exploration of the history of the sixteen locomotives.

It was quickly discovered that the class was not very well served in its documentation since such as did exist was usually in conjunction with other Southern Railway types and much was of a fragmentary nature and suffered from misconceptions, particularly in relation to details of the Bulleid alterations. Out of this was born this volume which is now offered as a record of a puzzling locomotive class which so often fell short of its theoretical potential.

Acknowledgments

Researching material for this volume has had its rewards and disappointments; one of the gratifying aspects has been the ready assistance afforded by many people when approached with queries or requests to search records. In particular the time-recording fraternity has taken untold trouble to put logs – poor, indifferent and good – at the author's disposal. Mr R. N. Clements has provided much data from his own notebooks as well as those of his deceased brother; Mr K. J. Baker has given details of runs noted by his late father, while Mr P. W. B. Semmens has kindly reproduced copies of running from the late Rev. J. H. Mortimer's records; Mr D. Maidment went to great pains to supply information on his post-war daily runs with the class and Mr Michael Hedges sent tabulations of most, if not all, of the runs he enjoyed or endured with the class; the running notes taken by the late F. E. Box came through the kindness of Mrs Bloxam in the form of Mr Box's notebooks which were in the possession of her late husband; useful data was also gathered from Messrs A. G. S. Davies and S. C. Nash. Thanks are also due to the editor of the *Railway Magazine* for allowing reference to runs which have appeared in that journal in past years.

Official records have been examined in the Public Record Office and the National Railway Museum, York, and information has been gleaned from Messrs H. C. Casserley, J. R. Fairman, B. Fletcher, G. D. Hinchliffe, J. N. C. Law, S. C. Nash, G. O. P. Pearce, S. C. Townroe and E. S. Youldon; the last-named gentleman in particular made valuable suggestions in regard to parts of the text. The task of reading right through the manuscript was nobly undertaken by Mr S. C. Nash who gave constructive advice and encouragement. To all concerned the author is pleased to express his indebtedness.

1

The Most Powerful Passenger Engine in Great Britain

Early in the life of the newly formed Southern Railway its Traffic Department declared its intention to operate 500-ton trains at an average start-to-stop speed of 55 mph. Since there was no existing locomotive able to do this a clear requirement was placed before the Chief Mechanical Engineer, R. E. L. Maunsell. Fortunately, apart from a move from Ashford to Waterloo, the CME of the new Railway was not faced with a vast organisational problem because he had been in charge of South Eastern & Chatham Railway locomotive affairs for a decade and had acceded naturally to the post in the larger Company; his main task was to weld the capacity of Ashford, Brighton and Eastleigh works into a harmonious whole.

By the time the move to Waterloo was made in 1924 two men had emerged as assistants who were to influence Southern Railway locomotive design – James Clayton and Harold Holcroft. Clayton carried Midland Railway ideas and had mixed with designers forming the Association of Railway Locomotive Engineers, while Hol-

croft hailed from Swindon with an interest in conjugated valve gears. He had propounded in 1920 a suggestion to set the cranks in a four-cylinder locomotive at 135 instead of the customary 180 degrees, which would produce a less uneven torque in pulling and more even blast on the fire by reason of eight exhausts per wheel revolution. He went to some pains to stress that the proposal was most suitable for heavy traction at slow speed and gave as his opinion that the ideal arrangement would be for the inside cylinders to drive the leading axle (in a 4–6–0 design) and the outside cylinders the middle axle. In 1922 Mr Hookham of the North Staffordshire Railway produced an 0–6–0 tank engine with four cylinders and the advocated crank setting but it was quickly rebuilt as a tender engine and was soon scrapped.

Maunsell resisted the temptation to rush out a new design and, when the Rolling Stock Committee authorised the immediate construction of twenty express passenger locomotives at its October 1923 meeting, the decision was taken to

1. This engine was used as a guinea pig to test the idea of an 135-degree crank setting which, in due course, became a notable feature of the Lord Nelson class. By the time this photograph was taken (October 1925) renumbering from E449 to E0449 had taken place.

use the LSWR N15 4–6–0 design, and initiate immediate improvements on that into what became the King Arthur class proper, and to make haste slowly with the completely new proposition.

Meanwhile Holcroft himself decided to check his theory; he took the last survivor of Drummond's 448–457 series of four cylinder 4–6–0s – no. E449 – turned the cranks of the inside cylinders through 45 degrees to obtain the desired eight impulses per revolution and rebalanced the wheels. Trials on goods trains conducted between Salisbury and Basingstoke indicated a

saving in coal consumption: so far as is known, the guinea pig engine was not tried on passenger duties to see if the saving was maintained doing that sort of work.

Following this experiment in April (before alteration) and May (after alteration) of 1924, the skeleton of the new locomotive was being roughed out. The 135-degree crank setting was accepted – very surprisingly because it had no particular advantage in an express passenger design – pending the confirmation of the tentative idea of a four cylinder 4–6–0, which would have to come within the 21-ton axle loading laid down by the Civil Engineer as the maximum allowable. The summer passed and it was October before Clayton had a footplate trip on GWR Castle class no. 4076 on the down 'Cornish Riviera Express', comparing the result ten days later to another footplate ride, this time on an LNER A1 class 4–6–2 on the down 'Flying Scotsman'. As a consequence, Clayton reiterated his earlier preference for the ten-wheel type and four cylinders, which was a logical conclusion to come to at that particular time. An added bonus was that four-cylinder engines found favour with the Bridge Stress Committee.

Little more happened until the next year when, with the basic points of wheel and cylinder arrangement settled, the driving wheel diameter had to be considered. Eastleigh works had a stock size of 6 ft 7 ins and there was no particular reason to depart from this. The boiler was to be fifteen feet long between tube plates and to have a Belpaire firebox. In the event a modification to 14 ft 2 ins was made to use the same tube length as on the King Arthur class and so avoid adding further to the range of items to be produced by Eastleigh. With the tendency for boiler pressures to increase with new designs, the figure adopted was 220 lb/sq. in., just below the 225 lb of the Castle but rather more than the 180 lb of the LNER Pacifics.

On 29 May 1925 an order was placed for fifteen more King Arthur class engines but, with the new design coming forward, this was amended three weeks later (17 June), under Rolling Stock Committee Order 124, to fourteen King Arthurs and one new 4–6–0 type, with a probable completion date of the end of June 1926.

Detailed design work proceeded and by the end of 1925 erection work had begun. The engine itself was forty-one feet long (only the GWR King ever exceeded this length for a 4–6–0) with a fifteen-foot rigid wheelbase. The outside cylinders of 16½ inches diameter × 26 inches stroke drove the cranks (set at right angles to one another) of the middle pair of coupled wheels while the inside cylinders (of the same dimensions as the outside pair) were placed 12 inches ahead of the outside cylinders and powered the leading pair of driving wheels, the

cranks again being set at right angles to one another but advanced 45 degrees relative to the outside cylinder cranks. Four separate sets of Walschaerts valve gear were employed rather than any conjugated gear favoured by Holcroft. To keep the weight down as much as possible the connecting and coupling rods and valve gear were made from Armstrong, Whitworth & Co's 'Vibrac' high-tensile steel, so helping to keep the balance weights required in the wheels to a low figure. The piston valve diameter was 8 inches with 1½ inches lap, 6½ inches travel in full gear and ¼ inch lead with cut-off in full gear 70 per cent. The last figure was increased to 75 within a few months of construction. Minimum curve radius for the engine was 6·52 chains.

The boiler, as noted, had a working pressure of 220 lb/sq. in. with a Belpaire type firebox, both new departures for Eastleigh: the centre line was 9 ft 2 ins above rail level and there were 173 2-inch diameter tubes and 27 5¼-inch diameter tubes, all 14 ft 3¾ ins long, with a Maunsell-type superheater with relief valves. The boiler was assembled from steel plate flanged by the North British Locomotive Co. The firebox had a grate 33 sq. ft in area (another high figure for a 4–6–0), flat at the back and sloping under the brick arch; the firebox water space stays were of steel within the fire area with nuts on the fire side and ordinary riveted copper stays elsewhere. Heating surface figures were (all in square feet):

Firebox	194
Small tubes	1282
Large tubes	513
Evaporative total	1989
Superheater	376
Total	2365

Tractive effort, at 85 per cent boiler pressure, worked out at 33,500 lb.

The cab had the luxury of one window each

side. Other equipment included a four-feed sight feed lubricator with separate condenser for cylinders and valve chests, a 'Diamond' soot-blower, Gresham No. 11 live steam injector (left hand) and Davies & Metcalfe No. 11 exhaust steam type F injector.

The weight of the locomotive was kept down to 83 tons 10 cwt with 20 tons 13 cwt on each driving axle, the adhesion factor being 4·15. The tender was a 'cleaned up' version of the bogie type attached to the King Arthur class, having flush straight sides (instead of a coping at the top), a coal capacity of 5 tons, a tank for 5,000 gallons of water and, with vacuum reservoirs prominent to the rear, weighed 57 tons 19 cwt. This gave a total weight of 141 tons 9 cwt for the engine and tender in running order. Without fuel and water the weights were 75 tons 16 cwt and 29 tons 12 cwt respectively.

Combined length overall for engine and ten-

der was 69 ft 9¾ ins, making it the longest locomotive on the Southern Railway (not even the Pacifics beat this until BR days when fitted with 6,000-gallon tenders) and also the longest 4–6–0 with tender ever to be built for use in this country. All this was costed at £9,510.

This then was the locomotive, numbered E850, that the directors saw – in works-grey livery – on their visit of inspection to Eastleigh works on 10 August 1926. Running in took place in this livery (without nameplates) from East-leigh on the Bournemouth route for about a fortnight, after which the engine returned to works for adjustments and for painting in the standard Southern Railway colours. When it re-emerged at the beginning of the third week of September it was complete with nameplates – 'Lord Nelson'; the most noticeable of the alterations which had been made was the exten-sion of the pipes from the cylinder drain cocks,

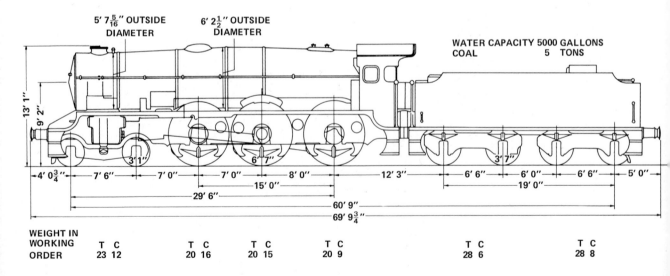

WORKING PRESSURE 220 LBS. PER SQ. IN.

2. Diagram of a Lord Nelson class locomotive.

from the cylinders to the leading edge of the steps immediately behind the front buffer beam.

On 27 September 1926 'Lord Nelson' made its debut at Waterloo, being assigned to Nine Elms shed for working ordinary passenger trains as trial trains to observe the engine's capabilities. Early in October it worked to and from Bournemouth and then 'The Most Powerful Passenger Engine in Great Britain' – as the posters issued by the Publicity Department proclaimed, taking tractive effort as the criterion – made its first appearance on the 'Atlantic Coast Express' on 12 October between Waterloo and Salisbury. Going down, the instruction to work to the 90-minute schedule was closely observed, 35 seconds being gained with the 392 tons (tare) train, with a maximum speed of 83 mph near Andover. On the return – again with 12 coaches (388 tons tare) – an 8½–minute late departure

from Salisbury presented an excellent opportunity for the new design to demonstrate its ability. The initial stage to passing Andover Junction was far from promising as 2¾ minutes were lost on the 22-minute schedule, despite 25 per cent cut-off and full regulator on the ascent of Porton bank where the speed was 37 mph. The arrears on scheduled time were reduced to 40 seconds by Basingstoke (passed in 42 mins 10 secs) and with 80 mph running following, Woking was passed in 61 mins 15 secs, Hampton Court Junction in 70 mins 15 secs, Clapham Junction in 79 mins 5 secs and the unchecked journey was concluded in 85½ minutes, 6½ minutes inside the schedule of 92 minutes. Better running before Andover would have made an on-time arrival possible and was a missed opportunity on what was billed as a demonstration run; the practice, in these early days, of having driver Francis of

3. No. E850 in shops grey livery and un-named about to make a tentative run from Eastleigh.

4. Rev. A. C. Cawston

Eastleigh drive the engine wherever it went, accompanied as necessary by a pilotman, might have been a contributory factor in this particular case.

On the Monday following this run, no. E850 was transferred to Battersea shed in order to be available at Ashford works for a visit by the Duke and Duchess of York on 20 October. On this occasion, driver Francis permitted the Duke to drive the engine from the works to the station! Having arrived on the Eastern Section, 'Lord Nelson' was tried on the Dover boat trains: at first it distinguished itself only by losing time although subsequently some improvement was made.

By December the locomotive had returned to Nine Elms. Further running under observation by the design staff took place but this time with local crews instead of driver Francis. Down runs

4. 'Lord Nelson', now decked out in green livery and carrying nameplates, calls at Brookwood on a local main line service during its first month or so in service.

to Salisbury were with light loads and the dislike of early arrivals inhibited the running other than to booked times: in the up direction the best run, although with only ten vehicles (316 tons tare), was on 3 December when a nine-minute late departure was completely recovered despite signal checks. Net time was in the region of 80 minutes with a maximum speed of 90 mph and an estimated coal consumption of $34\frac{1}{2}$ lb per mile.

Two days before Christmas, observation was switched to the down 'Atlantic Coast Express' between Salisbury and Exeter. It was an unfortunate trip punctuated by single-line working, two dead stands and one severe slowing for signals and, apart from an average 87 mph from

22

Chard Junction to Axminster (pass-to-pass) and the ability to restart an 11-coach train on Honiton's 1 in 80 bank from a dead stand, nothing of note was demonstrated. After the sojourn at Salisbury 'Lord Nelson' went back to Nine Elms and to the Salisbury and Bournemouth workings.

The concluding test run, for which the engine was fitted with an indicator shelter, came on Sunday 10 April 1927 in fine weather. The special 16-coach train weighing 521 tons tare (522 tons gross) left Waterloo at 8.52 am on a 90-minute booking to Salisbury which just

5. The first of the class had unique nameplates in that the class name was not carried (compare with Ill. 10).

5. Brian Morrison

23

6. H. C. Casserley

complied with the 55 mph standard for a 500-ton train. Again there were delays (a signal stop at Earlsfield where there was a diversion to the local line with a further slowing at Raynes Park in regaining the main line) and the actual time taken was 96¾ minutes, although the net time worked out just within the schedule set. Coal – good Welsh stuff – consumption was 66½ lb per mile.

West of Salisbury there was a schedule of 103 minutes to Exeter which included a minute's pause at Sidmouth Junction. The 87-minute booking from Salisbury to this stop fell a little short of the 55 mph average requirement. 'Lord Nelson' completed the run to Exeter with three-quarters of a minute to spare, having attained a maximum speed of 84 mph in the vicinity of Axminster and, on the climb to Hewish summit, returned the highest IHP figure – 1467 – of the trip.

6. 'Lord Nelson' at Nine Elms shed fitted with indicator shelter for test run purposes.

The test could hardly be said to have been very taxing and the opportunity to make up lost time was let slip. The return to London the same day was not part of the test proceedings.

Not long after this no. E850 was placed on exhibition (2–7 May) at Brighton Central in company with the old LBSC 'Gladstone', which had been saved for posterity by the efforts of the Stephenson Locomotive Society; a similar one-day joint exhibition was staged at Waterloo (platform 12) on 14 May. Next day 'Lord Nelson' was transferred to Battersea and began ordinary revenue-earning service on 16 May with the 11 am down boat train.

During a visit of the King and Queen of Afghanistan to England in the spring of 1928, the King had an engagement to visit part of the

Royal Navy's Atlantic Fleet, sailing in the flagship HMS *Nelson* from Portland to Portsmouth during the exercise. His Majesty's journey to Portland on 3 April was made by rail and fittingly 'Lord Nelson' was turned out to head the Royal Train of five Pullmans from Waterloo, with driver Francis at the regulator, as far as Weymouth Junction but not along the branch to Portland itself. For the 142¼-mile journey – the longest non-stop run ever made on the Southern – special authority was given to omit the compulsory halt at Poole by passing slowly. The schedule laid down was a pedantic one minute less than three hours which, coupled with the moderate load, provided none too exacting a task for 'Lord Nelson'. Although the King of Egypt had travelled in additional coaches attached to the 10.45 am departure from Victoria to Dover on 26 July 1927, this was the first, and by no means the last, Royal Train to be served by a Lord Nelson locomotive.

7. 'Gladstone' and 'Lord Nelson' side by side at Nine Elms in connection with the exhibition at Waterloo on 14 May 1927.

2

1928–31: Sir Francis *et al.*

Solitary express locomotives are more of an embarrassment to the Operating Department than anything else. Because of maintenance and overhaul demands, not even one prestige train can be accelerated to the power capability of the solitary locomotive if such capability is greatly above the level of the next-in-line of motive power units available. It was, therefore, pointless for the Southern operating authorities to knock a few minutes off the schedule of the 'Atlantic Coast Express' east of Salisbury or the premier continental express between Victoria and Dover (later to become the 'Golden Arrow') if the King Arthurs were not able to keep time on the occasions when 'Lord Nelson' was absent from duty.

Accordingly it was a foregone conclusion that, unless the design was a palpable failure, the class would be multiplied. So it proved, for as 'Lord Nelson' was nearing the conclusion of its tests – a series of trials, perhaps none too searching, lasting eight months – the Rolling Stock Committee meeting held at Waterloo on 17 March 1927 recommended that ten Lord Nelson type engines be built in lieu of ten King Arthur units then on order from Eastleigh works.

The first of this order (Rolling Stock Committee Order 157), no. E851, 'Sir Francis Drake', made its appearance in June 1928 and the tenth

engine was completed in April 1929 just in time for the 'Golden Arrow' train which was introduced the following month – although, by an odd coincidence, this tenth locomotive seldom worked on the Eastern Section of the Southern. Each of the locomotives was costed at £7,765 and carried the name of a notable sea-dog as follows:

E851	'Sir Francis Drake'
E852	'Sir Walter Raleigh'
E853	'Sir Richard Grenville'
E854	'Howard of Effingham'
E855	'Robert Blake'
E856	'Lord St Vincent'
E857	'Lord Howe'
E858	'Lord Duncan'
E859	'Lord Hood'
E860	'Lord Hawke'

These were good enough sounding names, except possibly for the fourth, which smacked of an estate agent in the Surrey stockbroker belt.

One or two amendments to the design as introduced by 'Lord Nelson', although not apparent to the casual observer, were made in this batch. These included laminated springs for the bogie wheels instead of the helical type on no. E850 and modified lead of the exhaust steam to the base of the blastpipe.

Rather more significant modifications were incorporated in the last two of the order: it had been proposed to try 6 ft 0 in diameter driving wheels for work on the Eastern section, but in the event this alteration would have been too radical without making compensating alterations to standard dimensions and the compromise of 6 ft 3 ins was adopted. This had the

8. No. E852 passing Folkestone Junction with the up Dover boat train. This engine and no. E853 were initially fitted with six-wheel tenders.

8. National Railway Museum

9. H. C. Casserley

10. Brian Morrison

effect – on a formula basis – of raising the tractive effort (at 85 per cent boiler pressure) to 35,298 lb but in practice no noticeable benefit accrued, doubtless because the four-inch reduction in diameter was so slight. No. E860 was equipped with the longer boiler originally proposed for the class. According to Holcroft's understanding of the matter this was to see 'if steaming could be improved'. If this indeed was the case this defect was recognised at an early stage by the Southern design team. This boiler (also numbered 860) was 10 inches longer than the standard type and

was readily identified when fitted by the absence of the 'piano front' cover to the inside cylinders in front of the smokebox. The small tubes had an area of 1359 sq. ft, the large tubes 544 sq. ft and the superheater 399 sq. ft for a total of 2496 compared with 2365 sq. ft of the other members of the class. The engine weight rose by 1 ton 6 cwt. None of these modifications affected the book cost – at least in theory.

The tenders acquired by these ten engines were something of a mixed bag; whether this arose initially because in altering the order from the King Arthur to the Lord Nelson type the different design of tender was overlooked is not clear. Anyhow, nos E852 and E853 got 4,000-gallon, flush-sided, six-wheeled tenders and others had 5,000-gallon bogie tenders (of two types) from S15 class nos E828–37, although not

9. Rear view of the six-wheel tender which was fitted to no. E853 with the numberplate prominent in the centre of the end panel.

10. The standard type of nameplate carrying the class name and with half-height letters for the name title.

11. 'Lord Duncan', as fitted with Urie-type eight-wheel tender, near Petts Wood in March 1929.

11. H. C. Casserley

in numerical sequence. This resulted in nos E851 and E854–7 acquiring flush-sided tenders and nos E858–60 being paired with the Urie pattern.

With eleven engines available, nos E851–9 were allocated to the Eastern Section at Battersea and nos E850 and E860 were put to work in the summer of 1929 on the 'Atlantic Coast Express' right through to Exeter, no. E850 being shedded at Exmouth Junction for the purpose and no. E860 at Nine Elms. The Exmouth Junction locomotive worked the up train on Mondays, Wednesdays and Fridays, returning with the down train Tuesdays, Thursdays and Saturdays, with the Nine Elms engine on the balancing duty. The working was continued into the winter timetable but was not repeated in the following summer.

The Salisbury men did not take to the design and cited as objections the large diameter of the driving wheels for the Salisbury–Exeter road and the long boiler. The first of these dislikes overlooked the fact that the King Arthurs, from which such good running was obtained on this route, had no difficulty with the identical driving wheel diameter and the other objection was only valid in the case of no. E860. More to the point probably was that the men did not like attending to two inside cylinders and, finding the performance on the road not markedly superior to the N15 class 4–6–0s, saw no advantage in the larger machine. No attempt was made to try no. E859 with its smaller diameter wheels on the route and the experiment was allowed to lapse.

This reticence on the part of enginemen to take to the design was not confined to the west of England because the management sent a Nine Elms driver across to the Eastern Section to

12. The long-boilered no. E860 running light to the shed after reaching Exeter Queen Street with the down 'Atlantic Coast Express'. It clearly displays the vertical front under the smokebox which was peculiar to this locomotive at that time.

13. When the first eleven locomotives were fitted with smoke deflectors the two middle lamp irons were raised as this photograph of no. E851 at Dover Marine in September 1930 clearly demonstrates.

13. LCGB (Ken Nunn Collection)

show how to handle the class. Such a ham-fisted approach, even in the days of depression and the current climate of industrial relations, was unfortunate: one can readily sense the partisanship with which the Western Section tutor would be greeted and the obduracy resulting from having to accept instruction from a South Western man. Curiously, it was a reflection not only on management techniques but also on design shortcomings.

Fitting of smoke deflectors started with no. E850 in mid-1929 and progressed as the other ten locomotives passed through works. On 4 July 1929 no. E860 was spared from its 'Atlantic Coast Express' activities to work a trial run of the new 'Bournemouth Limited' from London to Bournemouth but this was not to presage regular haulage by the class when the public

two-hour service began on 8 July.

Meanwhile a further order (RSCO 348) had been placed in March 1928 for five more examples of the class – as against the fifteen requested – and in September 1929 the first of these was put into traffic to be quickly followed by the remaining four at a cost, in each case, of £7,295. This batch was complete in the November and names were allocated thus:

E861	'Lord Anson'
E862	'Lord Collingwood'
E863	'Lord Rodney'
E864	'Sir Martin Frobisher'
E865	'Sir John Hawkins'

14. Exhibit 12 at Wavertree Park, Liverpool in September 1930 was outwardly 'Lord Nelson' although, in fact, it was no. E861 'Lord Anson' in disguise.

14. LCGB (Ken Nunn Collection)

These five engines followed the standard design of nos. E851–8, except that all were equipped with smoke deflectors at the time of construction and standard flush-sided 5,000-gallon bogie tenders as fitted to 'Lord Nelson' itself.

The Lord Nelson class was to become rather lucky in that potentially dangerous accidents involving the engines would result in no more than slight damage and little hurt to life or limb. The first of these occurred on 23 January 1930 when no. E853 became partly derailed while approaching Kent House station on the outskirts of London and then re-railed itself, the train crew being completely oblivious to the whole affair until arrival on time at Victoria!

The train concerned was the 12-vehicle 'Golden Arrow', leaving Dover Marine at 4.57 pm,

which was running slightly late with driver Chapman of Battersea trying to make up arrears. At 6.23 pm, when passing through the up-facing junction at Kent House, the leading and middle driving wheels of the locomotive became derailed; the middle wheels appear to have been re-railed at the crossing a few feet further on but 880 yards were covered before the leading wheels re-railed themselves at the trailing junction, leaving in their wake 117 broken fishbolts, 11 damaged chairs, one smashed sleeper, one damaged crossing, three broken insulators and about 850 dislodged or damaged keys. Damage to rolling stock was minimal and to staff, pas-

15. A chimney without a capuchin circulated amongst the class prior to 1940 – here no. 856 is saddled with it. Note also the lamp irons on the smokebox door and the omission of the 'E' prefix to the number.

16. One of the pre-war exhibitions for which there always seemed to be a spare Nelson available – no. 862 at Barnes in September 1932.

sengers and bystanders nil.

A speed of between 50 and 55 mph (instead of 40 mph) coupled with considerable side wear on the leading driving wheels, the locomotive having run 57,000 miles and being due for repair at a mileage of 65,000, were the major causes thrown up by the inquiry into the accident. Points recommended for consideration included deeper wheel flanges, lubrication of check rails and increasing the strength of the bogie control springs.

In the course of the report it was stated that driver Chapman had had charge of this particular engine for the whole 17 months of its existence; with the mileage given above it may be deduced that on average twenty round trips from London to Dover were made every month. No. E853 was fitted with a six-wheel tender which had confined its use to the Eastern Section

but on going to works for repair after the accident it parted with that tender and was furnished with a Urie-pattern bogie type instead.

When the boat train traffic declined in the early 1930s the total locomotive allocation of Battersea diminished and that at Nine Elms grew although usually there would be more engines on the Eastern Section than the Western. There were frequent changes of allocation of individual engines between the two depots, the only exceptions being nos E852 and E853 which, during the period of their attachment to six-wheel tenders, remained constantly at Battersea.

Some alterations were made in these early years of the class to the lamp irons, first in

17. The small driving wheel variant of the class, 'Lord Hood', on exhibition at Sutton in September 1934.

18. Tender exchange caught at Bromley South in July 1935.

replacing the old type on no. E850 with the new standard Southern pattern and then, when smoke deflectors were introduced, by raising those at mid-smokebox level to slightly above the top edge of the deflectors. With route discs in this last position the driver's vision was partly obscured, so the two offending lamp irons reverted to (were re-sited to, in the case of nos E861–5 as these had deflector plates when built) their original height above rail level – just below the horizontal centre line of the smokebox – but were moved inwards and fixed on the smokebox door.

The six-wheel tenders of nos E852 and E853 were replaced by the Urie-pattern bogie type in 1930 and these in turn, also with the similar ones attached to nos E858–60, were replaced during 1931–2 by the flush-sided bogie pattern, thus producing uniformity in tenders which were numbered 1000–16 for the class. In 1931 the E prefix to the numbers, denoting an engine allocated to Eastleigh for repairs, was dropped. This prefix did not appear on the front buffer beam of members of this class when turned out new but did so following a policy change in 1930.

No. E861 temporarily changed identity with Lord Nelson in the autumn of 1930 and went up to Liverpool where it was exhibited at Wavertree Park, in company with other locomotives, as part of the Liverpool and Manchester Railway centenary celebrations (13–20 September).

Early in 1931 the cinema organist, Reginald Foort, took apparatus to record footplate sounds on to a Lord Nelson hauling a West of England express to obtain suitable noises which he could reproduce on the Wurlitzer at the Regal cinema, Marble Arch, London in his making of a record of the descriptive musical piece, 'Chou Chou'. Where, one wonders, is that recording today, for it must have been one of the first taken of footplate sounds in motion.

3

1932–7: Maunsell's Modifications

By 1932 the class could be said to be established. It was not, however, a very notable establishment; perhaps there was no need to improve the schedules but, whatever the reason, the level of Lord Nelson performance was not noticeably higher than that of the King Arthurs and at times gave rise for concern. Because there were but 16 instead of 26 locomotives, as intended at one time, there were not enough units to form two links, so a few odd engines were working on the Western Section while one link was formed at Battersea; the radius of action was extended during 1932 as the programme of strengthening bridges and permanent way had been completed to allow the class to run from London to Margate and Ramsgate via Faversham.

Mechanical reliability was also far from outstanding. In 1932 this class of 16 engines returned 16 mechanical failures for the year. This ratio of one for each unit was well above average for Southern locomotives: by way of comparison the King Arthurs had 37 failures for 74 units, the S15 class 4–6–0 13 failures for 35 engines and the Schools 6 for the 10 locomotives then built. Furthermore, the Lord Nelson record of eight boiler failures due to tubes leaking was

the worst for any class on the railway. The King Arthur group, for example, had six and that for well over four times as many units at work.

Perhaps 1932 was not a happy year for the Southern's premier class. At least it appears to have been recognised that the potential that the design should have had was lacking to some degree, and slowly some experimental alterations were made to some members of the class. First of all, at the end of 1933, no. 865 had its cranks altered to the traditional setting of 90 degrees from the 135 degrees standard for the class, making the engine readily identifiable audibly by its four exhaust beats per revolution instead of the unique eight. Visual identification could be made by the alterations to the weights in the driving wheels, which were noticeably ugly in comparison to the original design. Little or no advantage appears to have stemmed from this alteration but the engine remained in this condition for the remainder of its existence. Its reputation of being heavier on coal bore out the original thinking at the time the 135-degree setting was decided for the class.

The next modification concerned no. 862, which left Eastleigh works on 16 August 1934 fitted with a double chimney and modified Kyl-

19. The ugly balance weights in the driving wheels of no. 865 were the visual indication of the alteration of the cranks to the traditional 90-degree setting.

chap twin exhausts. The Kylchap exhaust had been evolved in France by M. Chapelon who adapted work undertaken by Kylala in Finland: the example fitted to no. 862 was of in-line type built up from sheet metal in three sections and each exhaust was of 1 ft $4^1/_8$ in. diameter at the top with a choke diameter of 1 ft $1\frac{3}{4}$ in., the two blastpipe orifices each being $4\frac{3}{4}$ in. diameter. Unusually, the Kylchap fitment did not provide the expected improvement in performance, which gives ground for thinking that there was some shortcoming in this particular example's design or application. If any further attempts were made to obtain rather better results (which seems doubtful), it was evident from observation of the running of no. 862 that little or no success attended such efforts.

A chimney without capuchin circulated among the class (presumably staying with the same boiler) and has been noted variously on nos 851, 856, 858 and 865 but it is not thought to have been associated with any particular exhaust trial.

Attention next passed to piston valve leads: the normal dimension, from the end of the head to the edge of the port, was ¼ inch and no. 852 was tried with this reduced to $^{1}/_{16}$ inch but, as from the early part of 1935, the dimension was standardised at $^{3}/_{16}$ inch for the class.

During the period covered by this chapter there was always an engine that could be spared to be put on exhibition if the occasion demanded. Judging by where some engines were displayed, the slightest opportunity appears to have been grasped; no. 862 turned up at Barnes in September 1932; no. 863 was exhibited at Brighton in December of that year just before the start of electric traction services there; no. 860 appeared at Portsmouth for Trafalgar Day 1933 and no. 859 was busy in 1934 visiting Devonport (from Exeter by way of the GWR main line) in August, Sutton in September and Exeter Central in December. Further Trafalgar Day exhibitions took place at Portsmouth in 1935 and 1936 in which nos 850 and 856 respectively participated.

The summer of 1936 saw new ground broken for the class when the agents' specials for boat traffic were diverted from Victoria to Cannon Street. Lord Nelsons had a Saturday duty which brought one of them up to Cannon Street and out again, the triangle at Borough Market and Metropolitan Junctions being used to turn.

In October of that year the 'Night Ferry' sleeping car service between London and Paris, using the newly constructed train ferries for the

20. Maunsell's exhaust experiments on the class were confined to fitting no. 862 with a Kylchap double chimney.

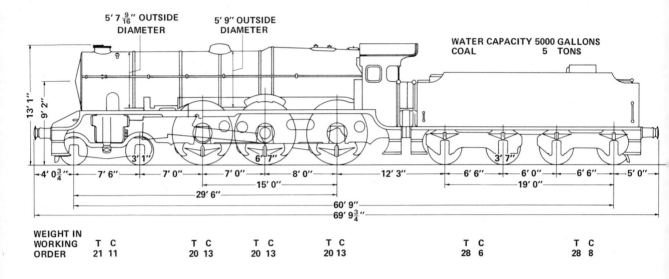

WORKING PRESSURE 220 LBS. PER SQ. IN.

5' 7 9/16" OUTSIDE DIAMETER

5' 9" OUTSIDE DIAMETER

WATER CAPACITY 5000 GALLONS
COAL   5 TONS

13' 1"
9' 2"

3' 1"   6' 7"   3' 7"

4' 0¾"   7' 6"   7' 0"   7' 0"   8' 0"   12' 3"   6' 6"   6' 0"   6' 6"   5' 0"
15' 0"   19' 0"
29' 6"
60' 9"
69' 9¾"

WEIGHT IN WORKING ORDER	T C 21 11		T C 20 13	T C 20 13	T C 20 13		T C 28 6		T C 28 8

21. Diagram of no. 857 as fitted with large boiler with round-top firebox.

sea passage, was inaugurated. The 500-ton trains were considered too heavy for the class to operate regularly – an unflattering decision seeing that the design had been evolved to work such a tonnage at 55 mph over the route concerned – so that double-heading by small 4–4–0 locomotives had to be resorted to. No. 854 was reported to have worked the train from Victoria on the second night of the service and a photograph of no. 855 hauling five coaches appeared in the *Railway Magazine* as 'the first sleeping car train from Paris to London'. In fact, this particular picture was of the second portion of the pre-inauguration special run on 12/13 October from Paris to London.

In January 1937 no. 857 was outshopped from Eastleigh works fitted with a taper boiler (no.

1063) having a round-top firebox and a combustion chamber extending into the barrel. This boiler, it was stated, was built with a view to gaining experience as to its suitability for a proposed Pacific design, although at the time some play was made of it being an improvement to the Lord Nelson class. The provision of the combustion chamber had the effect of shortening the boiler length between tube plates by 14 inches to 13 feet. The working pressure remained at 220 lb/sq. in. and a Sinuflo superheater was fitted in place of the Maunsell type. By using 2 per cent nickel steel plates the additional weight was kept within bounds. Comparative figures for standard boiler, longer boiler as fitted to no. 860 and this experiment are:

Boiler no.	Standard	860	1063
Length between tube plates	14 ft 2 in.	15 ft	13 ft
Outside diameter (maximum)	5 ft 9 in.	5 ft 9 in.	6 ft 2½ in.
Outside diameter (at front)	5 ft 7⁹/₁₆ in.	5 ft 7⁹/₁₆ in.	5 ft 7⁵/₁₆ in.
Heating surface (sq. ft)			
2–in. tubes*	1282	1359	979
5¼–in. tubes	513	544	628
Firebox	194	194	246
Superheater	376	399	460
Total	2365	2496	2313
Engine weight	83 tons 10 cwt	84 tons 16 cwt	85 tons 12 cwt

* Boiler 1063 had 1¾–in. and 2–in. tubes.

22. No. 857 with large boiler, a single snifting valve behind chimney and cranked smoke deflectors.

Only one pressure relief valve (commonly referred to as a snifting valve) was fitted and this immediately behind the chimney. The smoke deflectors were cranked outwards (from a head-on view) to assist in forward vision for the crew. This larger diameter was probably the principal cause of rolling of the engine of which enginemen complained.

None of these alterations, with the exception of that to the piston valve lead, ever got applied to any members of the class during the Maunsell regime, nor did the as-built variations on nos 859 and 860. The longer boiler (no. 860) always remained attached in pre-war years to no. 860 – except for the first eight months of 1937 when it was spare – as did boiler no. 1063 to no. 857.

The impression is that there was little or no follow-up to any of these modifications and no directive from the top to do so. The premise has been put forward that this was a deliberate policy adopted by Maunsell to prove that whatever alteration was made to the Lord Nelson design it could not be bettered. This seems an uncharitable view because Maunsell does not appear to have been another Webb or Dugald Drummond. Perhaps the promise of retirement, coupled with ill health and the electrification programme, made the matter of little urgency in Maunsell's eyes.

Whatever the reason, by the summer of 1937 the class had two boiler variants in addition to the standard type, one locomotive with smaller diameter driving wheels, one with a varied crank setting and yet another with an exhaust variation – a splendid challenge to the autumnal advent that year of a new Chief Mechanical Engineer!

4

The Performance of the Maunsell Design

In view of the limitations on a solitary member of a class, which are discussed at the beginning of chapter 2, it is not surprising to find that the first record of 'Lord Nelson' on ordinary service trains was to a schedule designed for observance by engines of lesser power. Cecil J. Allen had his first trip behind the class early in 1927 and described the run at some length. He had asked the Southern Railway authorities for a footplate trip, so that he could comment on the locomotive's capabilities in the *Railway Magazine*, and had expected this to be between London and Salisbury. However, rather to his surprise, he was directed to Victoria for the 10.45 am boat train to Dover Marine and the result, somewhat abridged, appears in detail A of table 1. Banking assistance out of the London terminus was dispensed with and driver Stuckey produced a painstaking run which concluded a quarter-minute late at Dover. In the first 30 minutes the highest speed (at Kent House) was 48 mph and the maximum on the trip – 70 mph – was attained after one hour's running. The observer was at pains to stress the easy con-

ditions under which the engine was working and one senses that the Southern Railway missed a good opportunity for some free publicity in not promoting a more energetic run. The result was far removed from 500 tons at 55 mph standards.

Later a boat train link of these locomotives was established and the schedule reduced to 95 minutes. The results were disappointing: one sifts through logs without much reward and forms the impression that on a day-to-day basis even this initial record by no. 850 was not often equalled, let alone surpassed.

It must in fairness be said that the boat trains were not an easy, nor cheap, type of train for the recorder to follow and such trips that were made had usually to be taken in the course of a holiday journey. That stated, it seems extremely unfortunate (if there was good running to be observed) that these logs throw up late arrivals and inadequate performances over a long period of time – in fact during the remainder of Maunsell's reign. A brief analysis indicates the data available on the down boat trains with schedules of 90 and 95 minutes to Folkestone and Dover

43

respectively.

Loco. no.	Load tons gross	Actual net times in minutes Folkestone Junction sidings	Dover Marine
860	350	93¼/91	
855	350	93¾/93¾	
850	375		108/96½
852	425		98¾/95
857	430	97½/91	
858	445		102/98
855	460	93¼/93¼	

It is difficult to find much to say in mitigation of these performances because the schedules could not reasonably be termed anything other than moderate. However, in March 1939 Cecil J. Allen published details of a run, gathered by an unnamed recorder, of no. 857 carrying the large, round-topped boiler (but not fitted with Lemaître exhaust as Mr Allen claimed because this particular engine was not so equipped until the autumn of that year). This, as detail B of table 1 indicates, was a much better effort from all points of view and might well have misled Mr Allen into thinking that the engine had the new equipment. If this sort of running had been sustained in pre-1937 days the class would not have fallen under such a cloud, although it must not be overlooked that by the date of this run the performance on the railway generally was benefiting from the better-quality coal available.

Turning to the up direction, the running is worse rather than better. With efforts, if that be the right word, such as no. 864 with 305 tons taking 102 minutes net from Dover Marine to

23. 'Howard of Effingham' sets out for London to a backdrop of the white cliffs of Dover with a Continental Express. On these duties the performance of the class was seldom remarkable.

Victoria it is kinder not to subject the class performance to a close scrutiny but rather to turn to the couple of up runs in table 1 (details C and D). The first of these, helped by a moderate load, was an above-average run which paid the penalty in the form of signal checks in the London suburban area, while the other was remarked upon by Cecil J. Allen as being a rare occasion of a gain by one of the Lord Nelsons, which was a nice way of cloaking a run which had been just behind schedule for two-thirds of its duration and got in early by recovering time on the easy schedule of the final stage.

With these standards it is perhaps fortunate for the Central Section that the locomotives never worked any of its traffic. On the Western Sec-

Table 1. VICTORIA – DOVER MARINE

A	B	Detail	C	D
1927	–	Date	19 Sept. 1938	1933
850	857	Locomotive no.	851	863
14	13	Vehicles	11	14
432	412	Tare load (tons)	348	432
460	435	Gross load (tons)	365	465
C. J. Allen	–	Recorder	R. N. Clements	C. J. Allen

Mls	Sch.	m.	s.	Spd.	Sch.	m.	s.	Spd.	Station	Mls	Sch.	m.	s.	Spd.	m.	s.	Spd.
0·0	0	0	00			0	00		VICTORIA	78·0	95	94	46		94	07	
4·0	9	8	45	41	8½	8	37		Herne Hill	74·0		sigs			87	30	
5·7		12	00	31		11	54	29	Sydenham Hill	72·3		sigs			85	15	
10·0	18½	18	25	37		17	35		Shortlands	68·0		sigs			–	–	
12·6	23	22	15	30	22	21	18	31	*Bickley Jc.**	65·4		sigs			75	48	
14·9	26	25	41		27	25	16		ORPINGTON	63·1		68	25	75	72	58	67
17·6	32	31	05	33		29	57		Knockholt	60·4		65	59	50	70	08	38
						pws											
21·7		36	05	61		35	44		Dunton Green	56·3		60	46	66	64	49	57
23·2	39	37	45	45	37½	37	17		Sevenoaks T.H.	54·8	63	59	14		63	04	
		pws (2)															
28·1		43	40	25		41	44	78	Hildenborough	49·9		52	39	38	55	12	36
30·6	47	47	25	30	45½	44	03		TONBRIDGE*	47·4	51	48	33		51	25	
35·9	53	53	45	66	51½	49	22		Paddock Wood	42·1	46	42	44	65	46	17	70
43·0	60	60	15	70		55	20	75	Staplehurst	35·0		36	25	70	40	00	
46·3		63	10	61		58	00		Headcorn	31·7		33	39	78	37	12	74
51·5		68	05	67		62	30		Pluckley	26·5		29	34	76	32	38	68
57·2	73	73	25	66	72	67	24	70	ASHFORD	20·8	27	24	52	75	27	32	70
		pws	25														
61·5		78	40			71	09		Smeeth	16·5		21	18	72	23	45	
66·5	84	85	00		81½	76	01		Sandling Jc.	11·5	18	16	24	54	18	53	52
71·0		89	30			80	06		FOLKESTONE C.*	7·0		–			13	24	
72·0	89½	90	30		87	81	08		Folkestone Jc.	6·0		10	14	54	12	12	43
78·0	98	98	10		95	89	30		DOVER MARINE	0·0	0	0	00		0	00	
		94				88			Estimated net-time (mins)			88			94		

*Speed restriction

tion there were not enough members of the class to form a separate link; the tendency was to allocate available Lord Nelsons to the more testing duties, but by the end of 1929, with the full 16 locomotives in service, the Western Section duties had become established as the 'Atlantic Coast Express' right through to Exeter and the 4.50 pm Waterloo–Portsmouth service. There were seldom more than six of the class at work on Waterloo traffic so the spread over the three principal routes was somewhat thin.

So far as the 4.50 pm Portsmouth train was concerned it was rather an odd turn producing a variety of classes. Fortunately, in 1930 F. E. Box was using the train from time to time to return to his home at Guildford and so there is available not just one or two runs on the train but a good representative selection of about thirty, of which half were by Nelsons. Of all runs recorded the best was by no. 862 with 11 coaches in 35 mins 46 secs, the second best being by H15 class no. 477 (36 mins 22 secs) with the worst by U class no. A808 (41 mins 30 secs) and the second worst by a Nelson in 39 mins 53 secs, noted as being 'sluggish throughout'. In defence of the 2–6–0 it must be recorded that the following evening the crew had got the measure of the engine and stopped in Guildford station a few seconds over the 39 minutes scheduled.

Table 2 gives the aforementioned 1930 best and two other good efforts of 1931. Little comment is required: in detail C no. 865, on a stormy evening, entered Guildford rather slowly which might have been due to a signal check, while in detail A no. 862 did very well with a heavier load. The performances of those Nelsons concerned in Mr Box's records (nos 860, 861, 862 and 865) were adequate with few blemishes in contrast to the Eastern Section running; even so the work was virtually indistinguishable from that on the same train by King Arthur class engines.

46

Table 2. WATERLOO – GUILDFORD

Detail	A	B	C
Date	2 May 1930	14 April 1931	18 May 1931
Locomotive no.	862	861	865
Vehicles	11	9	9
Tare load (tons)	321	276	278
Gross load (tons)	345	295	300

Mls	m.	s.	m.	s.	m.	s.
0·0 WATERLOO	0	00	0	00	0	00
3·9 Clapham Jc.	7	05	7	05	7	10
7·2 Wimbledon	11	03	10	45	11	07
9·8 Malden	13	41	13	07	13	40
13·3 *Hampton Court Jc.*	17	00	16	16	16	57
17·1 Walton-on-Thames	20	23	19	35	20	11
19·1 Weybridge	22	18	21	33	22	00
21·7 Byfleet	24	37	24	02	24	14
24·3 Woking	27	16	26	51	26	54
24·8 *Woking Jc.**	27	58	27	35	27	37
26·3 Worplesdon	30	43	30	21	30	19
30·3 GUILDFORD	35	46	35	43	37	02

*Speed restriction

This same comment also applied to the 'Bournemouth Belle' duty, except that Nelson running did not vary between the eight-coach winter working and the 50 per cent heavier summer load. Thus the winter performance gave the impression of being downright poor whereas the fault lay in a leisurely timing of 90 minutes for the 79 miles. A couple of down runs are recorded in table 3 (details A and B) and both, curiously, by no. 860, the long-boiler engine, which tended to perform just slightly better than nos 861, 862 and 865 with which it shared the duty. Working of the locomotive was much the same on both runs: milepost 31 was passed at 49 mph on the first trip and at 51 mph on the second, with 66 mph maximum on both near Hook and 49 mph and 76 mph at Woking and Winchester respectively – again on both runs. The two minutes dropped in detail A at the first relaying check remained a deficit throughout and it is odd that driver Burden of Nine Elms failed to regain any of that lost time: it would seem to indicate that the locomotive had nothing in reserve. Beyond Southampton there is no running worthy of record.

On the up journey data is again sparse. There are some runs with eight cars in 88¼ minutes unchecked and even one with six cars in 87¼ minutes which do not merit tabulation. The two runs which appear in table 3 present a contrast, as the first is of a heavy train which, incidentally, does get close to the 500 tons at 55 mph requirement, the second being of a light train powered by the locomotive with the Kylchap exhaust as fitted during the Maunsell regime. No. 853 recovered from the permanent way slack at Winchester Junction to 43 mph at Micheldever at which point no. 862 was doing 47 mph, while both engines bowled along in the high seventies

Table 3. WATERLOO – SOUTHAMPTON CENTRAL

	A		B		Detail		C		D	
	860		860		Locomotive no.		853		862	
	12P		12P		Vehicles		14		8P	
	471		468		Tare load (tons)		442		315	
	495		495		Gross load (tons)		470		330	
Mls	m.	s.	m.	s.		Mls	m.	s.	m.	s.
0·0	0	00	0	00	WATERLOO	79·2	91	15	82	47
3·9	7	48	7	13	Clapham Jc.	75·4	84	18	75	27
	pws									
7·2	12	53	11	44	Wimbledon	72·0	80	23	71	47
							pws			
12·0	19	05	17	00	Surbiton	67·2	74	03	67	27
19·1	26	03	23	36	Weybridge	60·1	68	07	61	52
24·3	31	10	28	33	WOKING	54·9	64	12	57	51
28·0	35	09	32	33	Brookwood	51·3	61	32	55	05
31·0	38	45	36	02	*Milepost 31*	—	—		—	
36·5	44	24	41	58	Fleet	42·8		—	48	29
42·2	49	54	47	35	Hook	37·1	50	25	43	50
47·8	55	07	52	54	BASINGSTOKE	31·4	46	05	39	00
50·3	57	47	55	46	*Worting Jc.* *	29·0	43	57	36	10
—	—		—		*Litchfield S.B.*	22·9	37	30	sigs	
58·1	66	13	64	18	Micheldever	21·1	34	55	26	36
							pws			
66.6	73	20	71	09	WINCHESTER	12·7	20	05	16	50
	pws									
73·6	81	38	77	10	Eastleigh	5·7	11	25	9	25
	pws									
77·3	85	42	80	47	St Denys	1·9	5	45	—	
78·2	87	08	82	18	*Northam Jc.* *	—	—		—	
79·2	89	45	85	09	SOUTHAMPTON C.	0·0	0	00	0	00
	85¼		85¼		Estimated net-time (mins)		86¼		80¾	

*Speed restriction

between Basingstoke and Surbiton with no. 853 getting a maximum of 83 mph approaching Woking and the other engine (with driver Delve in charge) touching 80 mph at Brookwood.

Next there is the Exeter road to be considered. For the first half – from London to Salisbury – data is relatively prolific, especially in relation to 'Lord Nelson' in early days before the class multiplied. However, it is all pretty mundane stuff such as the 89½ minutes of the press demonstration run with 392 tons tare (which seems to have been a deliberate timekeeping effort) and so the choice of runs has been made from the 1934–7 period when the memory of the 1927 Sevenoaks accident had dulled a little and the condition of the track had improved, so encouraging a rather more positive approach to running.

In detail A of table 4 no. 856 did well enough, with two permanent way checks to contend with, to get down to Salisbury in 89 minutes, the finish being a rousing affair taking as it did less than 1¾ minutes from passing Tunnel Junction to stopping in Salisbury. The same locomotive in detail B got frisky around Andover Junction to make amends for a tardy recovery from signal checks at the start of the journey. In detail C no. 862 (by then fitted with Kylchap exhaust arrangement) suffered a pair of moderate slacks

24. The 'Golden Arrow', from its inception until 1939, was a regular duty for the Lord Nelsons – here, in August 1931, in its all-Pullman days, no. 851 is in charge. Note the absence of 'No.' on the front buffer beam.

Table 4. WATERLOO – SALISBURY

Detail		A			B			C			D		
Locomotive no.		856			856			862			857		
Vehicles		13			13			11			12		
Tare load (tons)		398			420			356			388		
Gross load (tons)		425			450			375			420		
Mls	Sch.	m.	s.	Spd.	m.	s.	Spd.	m.	s.	Spd.	m.	s.	Spd.
0·0 WATERLOO	0	0	00		0	00		0	00		0	00	
						sigs							
3·9 Clapham Jc.	7	6	52		8	55		7	06		6	43	54
7·2 Wimbledon		10	43		13	32		11	12		10	38	55
			pws							35		pws	
12·0 Surbiton		17	06		18	43		16	43		15	34	49
19·1 Weybridge		24	30		25	21	61	24	52		22	13	68
									pws	20			
24·3 WOKING	28	29	26		30	19		30	19		27	44	58
28·0 Brookwood		33	11		34	11		35	32	54	31	05	62
31·0 *Milepost 31*		36	28	54	37	35	51	38	46	57	34	03	60
36·5 Fleet			—		43	10	67	43	41	73	38	50	68
42·2 Hook		47	09	70	48	32	69	48	24	77	43	50	68
47·8 BASINGSTOKE	52	52	13	64	53	38		52	53		49	01	60
50·3 *Worting Jc.*	55	54	45	55	56	11	54	55	10	61	51	45	54
55·6 Overton		60	05		61	35		60	01	71	57	16	64
59·2 Whitchurch			—		64	38			—	78	60	23	72
61·1 Hurstbourne		64	43	74	66	06	80	64	20	85	61	55	75
66·4 ANDOVER JC.	69	69	28	77	69	55	91	68	12	83	65	51	83
			pws										
72·7 Grateley		77	54	44	75	01	58	73	48	51	71	15	57
78·2 Porton		83	47	81	80	06	86	79	17	75	76	52	72
82·6 *Tunnel Jc.* *	84½	87	21		83	15		83	04		81	04	
83·7 SALISBURY	87	89	02		85	32		85	26		84	08	
Estimated net time (mins)			84			83½			80¾			83	

*Speed restriction

early on and then went on to win back all lost time by Andover Junction, after which matters were not pressed at all, an early arrival being assured. A splendid net time of 80¾ minutes resulted and for this some praise must surely be accorded to the double chimney fitment. The last of these down runs is Rev. J. H. Mortimer's record of the large-boilered no. 857 driven by Payne of Nine Elms. To hamper Fred Payne there was a slight permanent way check before Surbiton and, for some reason not readily apparent, the engine was eased slightly approaching Woking (possibly a cautionary signal sighted at a distance by the driver but not so observed by the recorder) but thereafter did well to go over the milepost 31 summit at the mile-a-minute rate. With so much time in hand the locomotive was kept in check after the excellent climb to

25. In pre-war days a booked Lord Nelson assignment was the Pullman 'Bournemouth Belle'. Here, no. 861 passes Walton-on-Thames with the down train in 1938.

Grateley. This was a good run with man and machine demonstrating complete mastery of the job.

Before dealing with the up runs from Salisbury it is convenient to consider working west of Salisbury. Sadly there is not much to consider. With the proliferation of the class, working west of Salisbury began in the summer of 1929 but did not prosper. It continued for a time – about a year or so – until the authorities decided that the class should confine its activities, so far as the west of England services were concerned, to east of Salisbury. This decision appears to have been helped by the attitude of the Salisbury enginemen.

In the period during which the few members of the class worked the traffic (principally nos 850, 860, 861 and 863), little materialised for recorders to get excited about. One non-stop run in each direction is tabulated for the record (table 5) and sections of the running give an impression of labouring, particularly in recovering from checks and uphill. The Lord Nelsons at times barely equalled, let alone bettered, the work that the King Arthur engines did on this route. It certainly appeared that the advantage that the larger machines had in theory could not be translated into practice and so the King Arthurs held undisputed reign for a dozen more years until the Pacifics completely eclipsed their efforts.

To round off this review of the work of the class in its original condition comes the Salisbury – Waterloo length, which probably saw the best work of all. Running in table 6 is opened by driver Payne and engine no. 861 with fireman Budd assisting in no small measure. This was a good run – exceptional, indeed, for the period – indicating a potential seldom exploited. The second effort, with the long-boilered no. 860, showed a close correspondence to the first, the net time again being assessed as $84\frac{1}{2}$ minutes.

Table 5. SALISBURY – EXETER CENTRAL

	A	Detail		B
	850	Locomotive no.		850
	12	Vehicles		11
	389	Tare load (tons)		340
	410	Gross load (tons)		360

Mls	m.	s.		Mls	m.	s.
0·0	0	00	SALISBURY	88·1	102	00
2·5	6	25	Wilton*	85·5	98	45
	pws					
8·3	15	55	Dinton	79·8	93	10
12·6	21	25	Tisbury	75·5	89	35
17·6	27	35	Semley	70·5	84	30
21·7	31	00	Gillingham	66·4	79	40
28·5	37	10	Templecombe	59·6	73	30
30·9	40	00	Milborne Port	57·2	70	25
34·6	43	15	Sherborne	53·5	64	00
					sigs	
39·2	46	45	YEOVIL JC.	48·9	54	30
41·4	48	50	Sutton Bingham	46·7	52	45
48·0	55	20	Crewkerne	40·1	47	15
49·8	58	05	Milepost 133¼	38·2	45	20
56·0	64	00	Chard Jc.	32·0	37	45
61·1	68	00	Axminster	26·9	32	40
64·4	70	30	Seaton Jc.	23·7	30	10
70·1	81	35	Milepost 153½	17·9	24	10
71·3	83	10	Honiton	16·7	21	50
75·9	86	55	Sidmouth Jc.	12·1	16	15
79·7	89	50	Whimple	8·4	11	20
85·2	93	45	Pinhoe	2·8	7	50
86·9	95	20	Exmouth Jc.	1·1	3	45
88·1	97	45	EXETER CENTRAL	0·0	0	00

	94½		Estimated time (mins)		96	

*Speed restriction

This same locomotive had earlier been credited with a net time of 79 minutes for the same journey and similar load; unfortunately details were not forthcoming of this report and it may have proved to be false or over-optimistic – it was certainly uncharacteristic for the time.

In detail C is Rev. Mortimer's record of the return of the run previously described in table 4, detail D, with the large-boilered no. 857 and

Table 6. SALISBURY – WATERLOO

Detail	A			B			C		
Date	23 July 1930			pre-Sept. 1931			31 May 1937		
Locomotive no.	861			860			857		
Vehicles	12			12			11		
Tare load (tons)	410			417			354		
Gross load (tons)	440			445			376		
Recorder	Rev. Mortimer			–			Rev. Mortimer		
Mls	m.	s.	Speed	m.	s.	Speed	m.	s.	Speed
0·0 SALISBURY	0	00		0	00		0	00	
1·1 *Tunnel Jc.*	3	45		3	30		3	30	
5·5 Porton	10	00	42	10	00	38	9	19	47
11·0 Grateley	17	05		17	25		15	44	
17·3 ANDOVER JC.	22	30	75	22	40	86	20	42	80
22·6 Hurstbourne	–			27	10	70	25	09	62
24·5 Whitchurch	29	45	59	–			26	57	61
				sigs					
28·1 Overton	32	50	62	36	10		30	31	59
35·9 BASINGSTOKE	40	00	78	44	05		37	46	75
41·5 Hook	44	20	75	48	15	85	42	03	75
47·2 Fleet	48	25	78	52	40	80	46	36	76
55·7 Brookwood	55	10	80	59	30		53	30	76
59·4 WOKING	58	00	80	62	20		56	54	54
62·0 Byfleet	60	05	78	–	–	80	59	16	72
64·6 Weybridge	–			66	20		61	26	68
70·4 *Hampton C. Jc.*	–			–	–	70	66	15	69
							sigs		
71·7 Surbiton	68	20		72	20		68	47	
76·5 Wimbledon	73	10		76	55		75	52	60
79·8 Clapham Jc.	77	30		80	25		79	17	
	sigs			sigs			sig. stop		
83·7 WATERLOO	86	30		91	00		89	00	
Estimated net-time (mins)	84½			84½			82½		

driver Payne at the regulator. Once again there is an unexplained easing of the engine on the approach to Woking as if the driver was expecting a signal caution. Eventually there were signal checks but, despite slowings and a halt, Waterloo was reached 'right time'.

This final run does get into the 60 mph start–stop category for a net time, as do three runs in the down direction, although all miss an actual time to meet that requirement.

5

1938–9: Bulleid's Busy-ness

Upon the comparatively small class in September 1937 came the whirlwind in the shape of the new Chief Mechanical Engineer. Immediately upon his arrival Mr Bulleid got to grips with the motive power situation and even in the first month of his tenure experienced poor steaming with a Lord Nelson engine! However, he was not exactly a complete stranger to the design because ten years previously he had ridden on the footplate of the doyen of the class between London and Dover (when he had been an observer at the trials arising out of the Sevenoaks accident) and had noted difficulty in firing, poor visibility and the excellent riding qualities of the tender which added to the fireman's work because the coal failed to be fed forward by vibration.

Proposals for modifying the tenders were in existence and not unnaturally Bulleid, recalling his observations of a decade before, had the plans implemented. So the first sign of activity of the new regime that came to public notice was in November 1937 when no. 852 left Eastleigh works after an overhaul with a high-sided tender. This modification involved extending the side sheets upwards and inwards for the length of the coal void to compensate for the space lost internally by insertion of metal sheeting to give surfaces which would cause the coal to be self-trimming. The external appearance of not only the tender but the whole ensemble was enhanced, giving the effect of a more modern image compatible with practice then current on other railways in the country. The weight of the tender was increased by 1 ton 5 cwt although the fuel capacity remained unaltered. General application began with no. 855 in August 1938 and was eventually completed with no. 863 at the end of 1940.

At the same time that no. 855 had a modified tender attached it was fitted with a Flaman-type speed recorder which, in addition to giving an instant visual indication, took a continuous record of the speed on a roll which could later be removed for examination as required. These recorders, connected to the right-hand rear coupled wheel, were very rapidly acquired by the whole class over a period of about six months, with the exception of two which were fitted in June 1939 and the last one, on no. 860, in December 1939.

Neither of these innovations, of course, had a direct effect on the performance of the locomotives any more than did the livery

changes which were noticeably taking place at the time or the fitting, to no. 852, of a cab window washer and wiper which was the forerunner of those introduced many years later on road vehicles (except that road vehicles rely on cold water). This particular piece of apparatus consisted of a wiper blade and actuating unit, a sprayer to eject hot water on to the window, a control valve and a connection from the boiler feed pipe between injector and clack box. When the driver opened the control valve the action was entirely automatic. The date of fitting was November 1937, the same time as the engine acquired its high-sided tender.

Another early alteration made by Bulleid was for no. 858 to have the right-hand injector – a Davis and Metcalfe 10 mm class H exhaust steam type – replaced by an 11 mm 'Monitor' live steam type in the interests of easier operation and maintenance. This substitution was made in February 1938 and down the years various other types were used for the right-hand side, such as the Davis and Metcalfe 10 mm class J (no. 851), the same manufacturer's 11 mm class H (nos. 852 and 853) and the Gresham & Craven 11 mm RCW type (no. 856) in addition to the 'Monitor' on nos 864 and 865.

Attention was called for by the Sinuflo superheater incorporated in the round-top boiler fitted to no. 857; accumulations of ash occurred in the combustion chamber due to a disproportionate amount of flue gases passing through the superheater tubes at the expense of the small tubes in the lower part of the boiler. The fitting of one of the standard superheaters quickly eliminated this fault which was peculiar to the Sinuflo type.

However, Bulleid did not confine himself to external and minor improvements for, like so many locomotive engineers before him –

26. Two members of the class – nos 852 and 855 – had their tenders modified while still in the old livery. No. 855 passes Bromley South in August 1938 in this condition; it also carries the Flaman recorder apparatus, part of which can be seen near the rear driving wheel.

27. O. V. Bulleid fitted no. 865 experimentally with a Kylchap double chimney which was distinguishable from that on no. 862 by not having a capuchin. No. 865, thus equipped, passes Whitchurch with the down 'Atlantic Coast Express' in April 1938.

including Brunel and Gooch who had had their problems with poor steaming of 'North Star' – he turned his attention to the blastpipe and chimney. Late in 1937 and for the greater part of 1938 the matter came under extended examination: the standard blastpipe fitment for the class was one of $5\frac{1}{2}$ inches diameter having a cross-sectional area of 23·75 sq. ins with one variant in no. 862 which had for some years been carrying the Kylchap double exhaust and double chimney although without any particular advantage.

The first amendment was to reduce the blast-pipe orifice to 5 inches diameter and this appears to have been coupled with an adjustable two-piece cowl within the standard $18\frac{3}{4}$-inch diameter chimney, reducing the effective diameter to 13 inches. This cowl was made up from $1/8$-inch steel plate and its inner section, though tightly fitting, was adjustable to give various settings within a range of $4\frac{3}{4}$ to $14\frac{3}{4}$ inches from the lowest point of the bellmouth of the cowl to the centre line of the smokebox. The desired position had to be set laboriously by hand in the smokebox which underlined the empirical nature of the tests. Nos 852, 856, 860, 861, 864 and 865 were the engines involved in this experiment.

28. At the beginning of his exhaust experiments Bulleid tried no. 863 with a large stovepipe chimney but without a multiple jet exhaust. Still in the old livery, it is pictured in that condition approaching Andover Junction with the up 'Atlantic Coast Express'.

Next, in March 1938 no. 865 was fitted with a double chimney, again based on the Kylchap principle but without intermediate liners, each blastpipe being 5 inches diameter and fitted with three nibs giving a cross-sectional exhaust area of 32·2 sq. ins. The discharge from each cylinder was into one particular blastpipe (and chimney) rather than spread into both blastpipes. No. 862 was taken into works and had the intermediate liners to its original Kylchap exhaust arrangement removed and the blastpipe orifices altered from $4\frac{3}{4}$ to $4\frac{1}{2}$ inches diameter, giving an area of 31·8 sq. ins. Unlike no. 865 the orifices on no. 862 were plain.

Tests were conducted for ten days for each type on the Bournemouth line in the early summer of 1938, from which it was concluded that both engines performed better than the original design, although the advantage was with no. 865. In some respects it was a pity that no. 865 was involved in the experiment because this was a non-standard example in any case and was usually crewed by an exceptional pair of enginemen. For what it is worth, it is understood that no. 865 was heavier on coal to the tune of about 4 lb per mile more than no. 862 on these 12-coach service trains but only dropped time once (by reason of an out-of-course stop) whereas no. 862's performances showed an average debit of about $1\frac{1}{2}$ minutes.

Bulleid was not satisfied and so no. 863 became for a while a mobile test engine. It was turned out from Eastleigh at the end of June 1938 with a 23-inch diameter, rimless, stovepipe chimney and had the blastpipe cap removed completely to give an 8-inch diameter orifice and a cross-sectional exhaust area of no less than 50·2 sq. ins. The result in service was poor and official jemmies in the form of two $\frac{1}{4}$-inch diameter rods were placed across the top of the blastpipe at right angles to each other. This experiment did not lead to any improvement

and was abandoned; next, an inverted cone of 4 inches diameter was placed in the top of the blastpipe, giving an area of 36·5 sq. ins. No improvement resulted and so the empirical modifications were next switched to multiple-jet exhausts. By mid-November 1938 no. 863 was equipped with what in due course evolved into the standard fitment known as the Lemaître exhaust. Here it may be noticed that, contrary to popular belief, the large-diameter chimney was introduced before the multiple-jet arrangement.

The first of such arrangements involved seven jets, each of $2\frac{1}{2}$ inches diameter, one placed in the centre and the remaining six set around it in a ring discharging outwards at 1 in 12 giving a total area of 34·3 sq. ins. This turned out upon testing to be worse than Maunsell's original standard single blastpipe. Blocking off the central jet (area reduced to 29·4 sq. ins) did not get it up to the original design efficiency and so the next move was to five jets, still of $2\frac{1}{2}$ inches diameter, with an area of 24·5 sq. ins. The jets were next reduced to four in number but increased to $3\frac{3}{8}$-inches diameter; $3\frac{1}{8}$ inches diameter was next tried, then a $\frac{1}{4}$-inch diameter rod was fixed across the cap before reversion to five jets but of 3 inches diameter and back again to four at $2\frac{7}{8}$ inches diameter.

Meanwhile other members of the class (nos 855, 856, 861 and 864), in addition to no. 863, had been fitted with 23-inch diameter stovepipe chimneys and were engaged in the experiments. No. 856, for instance, was tried with five jets (at 1 in 27) of 3 inches diameter – later reduced to $2\frac{3}{4}$ inches – and no. 864 with five $2\frac{3}{4}$-inch diameter jets although with a larger (25-inch) diameter chimney. Variations with $2\frac{1}{2}$-inch and $2\frac{5}{8}$-inch diameter jets were made with no. 864.

Multiple-jet caps were also tried with a double chimney as well as with 15-inch chimney liners. The final result of all these experiments, and possibly others escaping record, was a circle of five jets each of $2^5/8$ inches diameter (giving an area of 27 sq. ins) inclined at 1 in 12 outwards, and a 25-inch diameter chimney which was manufactured from steel plate and welded together complete with rim. This became the standard fitting early in 1939, after twelve months of experimentation, and by the end of that year the whole of the class had the new equipment.

It should perhaps be noted that the true Lemaître exhaust incorporated a central jet which could be adjusted by the driver during running to sharpen the blast. Bulleid started with a central jet but soon abandoned it and it would be surprising, even for Bulleid who later proved himself not to be averse to innovation, if the idea of employing a variable central jet was ever seriously contemplated; although the French *mecanicien* might have revelled in the finesse of operation it afforded, his English counterpart would have regarded it as nothing more than a contraption to be ignored.

When no. 863 was launched on the exhaust experiments, modifications were made to the grate and to the ashpan in that the bars were spaced at greater centres and the airflow to the ashpan was improved: these alterations were

29. An interesting contrast at Stewarts Lane in 1939; by this time no. 863 (right) had been fitted with a multiple-jet exhaust but it had retained the stovepipe chimney, while no. 854 had acquired a modified tender and had the distinction of being the sole member of the class to receive the new-style lettering in conjunction with the original chimney.

30. A 'studio' picture of no. 864 showing the Flaman recorder which was fitted to the class in the 1938-40 period.

also applied to the other members of the class participating in the blastpipe trials. Later – and in some cases very much later – these grate modifications were made generally for the whole class.

Having dealt with the exhaust question to his satisfaction Bulleid next addressed himself to the cylinder layout. The original layout of cylinders and exhaust passages involved right-angle bends to carry the exhaust steam to the base of the blastpipe and Bulleid re-designed this area to cut down on frictional losses of live and exhaust steam by enlarging port areas and passages to make the flow of steam as easy as possible. His first essay into this field was with no. 851 which was fitted with new cylinders in June 1939. Owing to a misunderstanding no. 851 did not

have ten-inch piston valves fitted as Bulleid intended – and as became standard for the new cylinders fitted thereafter – but kept its eight-inch piston valves. This introduced yet another non-standard modification to the class because no. 851 remained in this unique condition until withdrawal. Identification of engines having the standard modified cylinders was made easy because the main steam pipe covers between the cylinders and smokebox no longer projected through the bottom of the smoke deflectors. Also, the blastpipe and chimney having been moved forward, the smokeboxes were lengthened and this did away with the distinctive 'piano front' by bringing the smokebox front into line with the vertical rise of the front platform. This feature had hitherto been confined to

59

nos 857 and 860 with their non-standard boilers.

An indication of the difference in areas brought about by these modifications is seen in the before and after cross-sectional areas (in each case in square inches) using figures for one piston valve, one set of steam and exhaust ports and passages and the blastpipe and chimney:

	Original	Modified
Steam port	24·8	35·5
Piston valve	50·3	78·5
Exhaust port	56	71
Blastpipe cap	23·75	27
Chimney choke	176·7	490·9

With these cylinder alterations steaming deteriorated and once again the exhaust arrangements had to be amended. At first the jet diameter was altered to $2^9/16$ inches and then, when the quality of coal could not be maintained at the improved standard instigated by Bulleid, it was further amended to $2\frac{1}{2}$ inches.

No. 857 became the first member of the class to receive the new standard cylinders in October 1939 followed by no. 860 in the December. Sub-sequent replacements continued into 1940 but the onset of hostilities put the brake on progress and with no necessity for fast running, together with the introduction of 4–6–2 types, the complete conversion of the class never came about.

During this time of change the sage-green livery which had been standard for the Southern Railway gave way to the lighter malachite-green, painted numbers on the cab side instead of on the tender, the disappearance of the cast number-plates on cab sides and the introduction of a new style of lettering which, in a few cases, was extended to the numerals on the front buffer beam of the locomotive. Running parallel with this experimentation for a while was another colour – olive-green – which a few of the class took as a mantle until the malachite-green had been finally chosen.

Throughout this period the division of the class was constant with ten locomotives at Stewarts Lane and six at Nine Elms: in July 1939, for example, nos 852, 858, 860, 862, 864 and 865

31. Exhaust arrangements of the class before (left) and after Mr Bulleid's modifications.

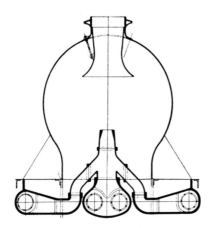

Fig. 1.—Original "Lord Nelson" exhaust arrangement.

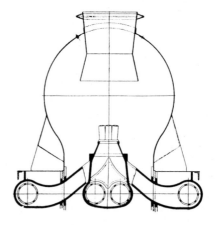

Fig. 2.—Exhaust arrangement with 10in. piston valves.

60

were at the Western Section shed. Of these nos 852, 860 and 865 were usually to be found on that section – indeed it is thought that no. 860 only once, for a short period, worked in Kent. Not only was the division constant but the duties also varied little: boat train traffic in the main occupied the Stewarts Lane contingent while the 'Bournemouth Belle' and 'Atlantic Coast Express' were the principal turns out of Waterloo with other expresses to Salisbury, Bournemouth and Weymouth making up the remainder of the work.

In the execution of the class's tasks the greatest improvement was undoubtedly on the Western Section; from this it should not be concluded that the performance on the Bournemouth and Salisbury trains had hitherto been in greatest need of improvement, for the contrary was the case, but rather that the peak of performance for the class was attained in 1939 by Nine Elms men and their half a dozen engines.

September 1939 was very much a watershed for the Lord Nelsons: not only were the inevitable demands of war shortly to be felt, but by then Bulleid had turned to his own designs, and that year saw the retirement of the redoubtable driver Payne, who had contributed so much to the making of the new reputation of the rejuvenated locomotives.

6

Performance Zenith

Bulleid's efforts to improve the work of the Southern Railway's 16 front-line express locomotives and the 40 members of the second rank was helped by the provision of better quality coal; by a raising of morale amongst, and the encouragement of the work of, enginemen; and by the introduction – on the Bournemouth line in particular – of trains in a new livery. All this might be considered as a harmonic of the outstanding locomotive work taking place on the routes to the north out of London, especially from King's Cross.

The fitting of no. 865 with a double chimney on Kylchap principles was followed by the series of exhaust experiments employing the Lemaître dictum. Once a solution had been obtained, the fixing of the equipment to the whole of the Lord Nelson class was rapid with all but two members being dealt with by midsummer 1939 (see page 116). On the other hand none of the class had received the new standard re-designed cylinders by the outbreak of hostilities in September that year. In examining the records of work performed by the class in 1938–9 it is important to ascertain within narrow limits when the running took place so that the precise condition of the locomotive concerned may be related to the work done.

On the Dover road there is again a lack of data, the sole example traced being that of no. 855 (with Lemaître exhaust) taking 417 tons (440 tons gross) down to Dover Marine in $93\frac{3}{4}$ minutes actual from Victoria with a net time of $90\frac{1}{4}$ minutes, which was work at a higher level than the route had seen generally but which was certainly not as good as the work of no. 857 with the large, round-top boiler noted previously in table 1, detail B. No. 855 passed Orpington in 26 mins 55 secs, Sevenoaks in 37 mins 28 secs, attaining 83 mph down Hildenborough bank, and was through Paddock Wood in $50\frac{1}{2}$ minutes before slowing for a permanent way check. Thereafter Ashford was cleared in $71\frac{1}{2}$ and Sandling Junction in 80 minutes; at no point was the work of no. 857 surpassed to any significant degree, no. 855 being no more than seven seconds faster between Headcorn and Ashford and but one second faster from Ashford to Dover Marine by which length no. 857 was in any case running easily.

On the Western Section the 'Bournemouth Belle' benefited at an early stage from the improvements made to the locomotives, as table 7 demonstrates. In detail A, which was a record made by Rev. J. H. Mortimer, no. 865 had the Kylchap exhaust as fitted by Bulleid and was crewed by driver Fred Payne and fireman Dunn. The recorder noted that there were 34 first-class

Table 7. WATERLOO – SOUTHAMPTON CENTRAL

Detail		A			B			C		
Locomotive no.		865			865			864		
Vehicles		10P			12P			12P		
Tare load (tons)		390			474			469		
Gross load (tons)		415			505			500		
Mls	Sch.	m.	s.	Speed	m.	s.	Speed	m.	s.	Speed
0·0 WATERLOO	0	0	00		0	00		0	00	
3·9 Clapham Jc.*	7	6	26		7	11	46	8	24	
7·2 Wimbledon		10	34	60	11	10	53	12	30	
12·0 Surbiton		15	25		16	00	64	17	17	
13·3 *Hampton C. Jc.*		16	36	68	17	10	68	–		
19·1 Weybridge		21	37	69	22	10	66	23	37	61
21·7 Byfleet		23	45	71	24	20	73	–		66
24·3 WOKING	29	26	02	67	26	37	65	28	33	
28·0 Brookwood		29	35	60	30	08	60	32	18	
31·0 *Milepost 31*		32	39	56	33	18	55	35	38	51
36·5 Fleet		37	45	65	38	38	65	41	07	
42·2 Hook		42	55	63	44	15	66	46	20	69
47·8 BASINGSTOKE		47	54	68	49	31	61	51	28	
50·3 *Worting Jc.* *	55	50	25	48	52	07	56	54	08	
58·1 Micheldever		59	03	73	60	13	67	62	25	
64·5 *Winchester Jc.*	70½	63	45	85	65	30			sigs	64
66·6 WINCHESTER		65	12	83	67	00	80	69	50	
						sigs				
69·7 Shawford		67	52	66	69	46	60	–		80
			sigs			sigs				
73·6 Eastleigh	79	71	13		74	31	20	75	32	
			sigs							
77·3 St Denys		75	49	15	78	51	60	78	37	
78·2 *Northam Jc.* *	84	78	30		80	30		80	02	
79·2 SOUTHAMPTON C.	87	82	09		83	47		82	42	
Estimated net-time (mins)		79			80¼			82		

*Speed restriction

and 157 second-class passengers. The running was resolutely excellent from the start but as so much time was being gained the locomotive could afford to be eased for Worting Junction and again at Shawford, neither of which easings could avert a severe signal check which was encountered in the last few miles; so the train pulled into Southampton five minutes early with a net time of, at most, 79 minutes which was within the mile-a-minute rate. The weather was fine without any wind.

No. 865 turns up again in detail B of this table in the same condition, although with a heavier load, and produces with the same driver another impressive performance, rather better from Clapham Junction as far as Brookwood, especially in relation to the load, paying the penalty again for early running in the Southampton area. The three-minute late departure from Waterloo had none the less been recovered. Last in this table comes no. 864 with the Lemaître fitment performing well enough in the hands of driver Delve (mainly on 18 to 22 per cent cut-off with adjustments on the regulator) but not so exhilaratingly as no. 865. All three runs show a marked superiority over work by the original design.

Table 8 records three runs on the up 'Bournemouth Belle' between Bournemouth and Southampton. The figures speak for themselves, and it is only necessary to remark that no. 865 had the Kylchap exhaust as fitted by Bulleid. No. 862 had either the Kylchap exhaust or, more likely, the Lemaître arrangement, while no. 863 certainly had the Lemaître fitting.

The review of running on the Bournemouth road is completed by table 9. Detail A is a con- tinuation of table 8, detail B, and the other log is of Lemaître-fitted no. 865. Both runs were excellent and better than had been seen previously with the unmodified type of engine. The climbing from Eastleigh up to Litchfield set new standards which were not to be regularly equalled until the Pacifics came on the scene some years later. The maximum short-term power outputs on these climbs were in the region of 1450 EDHP.

The Nelsons always appeared to be happiest on the Salisbury road and none of the runs now to be examined belies this. Table 10, detail A, another of Rev. Mortimer's timings, has no. 865 newly fitted with Kylchap exhaust, fine weather with a strong head wind to contend with, a one-minute late departure and driver Payne and fireman Whatley in attendance. There is no better Nelson run on this length on record – need

Table 8. BOURNEMOUTH CENTRAL – SOUTHAMPTON CENTRAL

Detail	A			B			C		
Date	7 Oct. 1938			–			6 Aug. 1939		
Locomotive no.	865			862			863		
Vehicles	8P			12P			12P		
Tare load (tons)	315			471			470		
Gross load (tons)	330			500			500		
Recorder	H. T. Clements			–			H. T. Clements		
Mls	m.	s.	Speed	m.	s.	Speed	m.	s.	Speed
0·0 BOURNEMOUTH C.	0	00		0	00		0	00	
3·7 Christchurch*	6	05	64	6	19	62	6	50	64
7·0 Hinton Admiral	9	50		9	45	47	10	10	47
9·5 New Milton	12	35		–			13	10	
12·5 Sway	15	25	64	15	53		16	25	55
15·2 BROCKENHURST*	18	05	69	18	33	71	19	10	70
20·0 Beaulieu Road	22	50	57	22	50	59	23	20	
22·6 Lyndhurst Road	25	20	64	25	24	64	25	50	65
26·2 Redbridge*	28	45		29	13		29	25	
27·9 Millbrook	30	45		–			sigs		10
28·8 SOUTHAMPTON C.	32	35		33	20		37	05	
Estimated net-time (mins)	32½			33¼			33½		

*Speed restriction

Table 9. SOUTHAMPTON CENTRAL – WATERLOO

Detail	A			B		
Locomotive no.	862			865		
Vehicles	12P			12P		
Tare load (tons)	471			462		
Gross load (tons)	500			495		
Mls	m.	s.	Speed	m.	s.	Speed
0·0 SOUTHAMPTON C.	0	00		0	00	
1·1 *Northam Jc.**	3	30		3	23	
5·7 Eastleigh	9	49		10	22	48
9·5 Shawford	13	58	56	14	52	52
12·7 WINCHESTER	17	20		18	24	53
14·7 *Winchester Jc.*		–		20	48	53
21·1 Micheldever	26	38		27	49	54
22·9 *Litchfield S.B.*	28	41	53	29	51	55
29·0 *Worting Jc.**	34	44		35	36	
31·4 BASINGSTOKE	37	04		37	49	76
37·1 Hook	41	51	72	42	21	72
42·8 Fleet	46	44	72	46	54	76
48·2 *Milepost 31*	51	30	66	51	26	70
51·3 Brookwood		–	70	53	52	75
		sigs				
54·9 WOKING	57	36		56	46	75
60·1 Weybridge	62	34		60	59	68
67·2 Surbiton	69	12		66	56	67
		sigs				
72·0 Wimbledon	73	50		71	13	69
75·4 Clapham Jc.	77	19		74	54	
79·2 WATERLOO	83	40		81	10	
Estimated net-time (mins)		82			$81\frac{1}{4}$	

*Speed restriction

more be said?

Both Rev. Mortimer and F. E. Box were recording the work of driver Payne and fireman Whetton with Lemaître-fitted no. 865 on 14 July 1939 (table 10, detail B) when a further excellent run was made. Four days later another Lemaître-equipped engine, no. 864, was engaged on the 'Atlantic Coast Express', this time with driver Delve (also of Nine Elms), who engineered an outstanding climb to Grateley (detail C). The same locomotive with the same modification reappears in the last run in this table and once again there was good climbing to

milepost 31 and up to Grateley and, with a two-minute late departure from Waterloo, the arrival at Salisbury three minutes behind time was no disgrace considering load and checks.

Detail A in table 11 relates to no. 852 when it was working with modified single blastpipe. The performance appears to have benefited to no small degree and with an unchecked run this particular engine would appear to have claim to the fastest actual (but not net) time from Salisbury to Waterloo. The second of the up journeys to be considered is the return of the trip recorded in table 10, detail A, with Kylchap-fitted no. 865

65

Table 10. WATERLOO – SALISBURY

Detail	A		B		C		D	
Date	12 May 1938		14 July 1939		18 July 1939		19 May 1939	
Locomotive no.	865		865		864		864	
Vehicles	11		12		12		14	
Tare load (tons)	354		387		388		453	
Gross load (tons)	376		415		415		485	
Recorder	Rev. Mortimer		F. E. Box		F. E. Box		R. N. Clements	
Mls	m. s.	Speed	m. s.	Speed	m. s.	Speed	m. s.	Speed
0·0 WATERLOO	0 00		0 00		0 00 sigs		0 00	
3·9 Clapham Jc.*	6 13	53	6 58		7 45 sigs		7 07	46
7·2 Wimbledon	9 55	59	11 25	52	12 26 sigs	30	11 14	55
9·8 Malden	12 23	65	14 08		16 05		pws	
12·0 Surbiton	14 25		16 16	65	18 31	58	17 39	
13·3 Hampton C.Jc.	15 42		17 29		19 50		—	
19·1 Weybridge	20 39	71	22 38	70	25 18	68	24 39	67
24·3 WOKING	25 22	61	27 18	64	30 09	60	29 28	59
28·0 Brookwood	29 00	59	30 48	62	33 53		33 07	61
31·0 Milepost 31	32 08	58	33 47	59	37 00	57	36 16	
36·5 Fleet	37 07	67	38 42	75	42 13	68	41 15	69
39·8 Winchfield	39 58	67	41 27	69	45 12	69	44 10	63
42·2 Hook	42 05	67	43 29	73	47 24	69	46 27	68
47·8 BASINGSTOKE	46 49		48 09	67	52 17	66	51 28	62
50·3 Worting Jc.	pws	33	50 30	60	54 42	58	54 02	55
52·4 Oakley	51 03		52 34	63	56 52	60	56 18	58
55·6 Overton	56 09	56	55 25	71	59 54	67	pws	
59·2 Whitchurch	59 22		58 22	73	62 55	75	64 20	62
61·1 Hurstbourne	61 04	76	59 53	77	64 24		66 10	69
66·4 ANDOVER JC.	64 57	86	63 53	86	68 13	86	70 28	82
72·7 Grateley	70 06	60	69 30	52	73 24	58	75 56	55
78·2 Porton	74 57	78 83	74 41 sigs	84	78 24	83	81 08	85
82·6 Tunnel Jc.*	78 27		80 02		81 53		84 34	
83·7 SALISBURY	80 20		82 17		83 48		86 55	
Estimated net time (mins)	78		80		81½		82½	

*Speed restriction

and driver Payne. An incentive provided itself in a 6½-minute late departure from which an absolutely splendid run ensued. Rev. Mortimer did not note that the strong headwind encountered going down had abated or moderated – indeed he makes no reference to weather conditions – so sceptics may latch on to the explanation of a strong tailwind. It was running of a calibre

Table 11. SALISBURY – WATERLOO

Detail	A		B		C		D	
Date	11 July 1938		12 May 1938		5 July 1939		17 July 1939	
Locomotive no.	852		865		865		851	
Vehicles	12		11		13		12	
Tare load (tons)	385		354		392		387	
Gross load (tons)	410		376		420		415	
Recorder	H. T. Clements		Rev. Mortimer		F. E. Box		F. E. Box	
Mls	m. s.	Speed	m. s.	Speed	m. s.	Speed	m. s.	Speed
0·0 SALISBURY	0 00		0 00		0 00		0 00	
1·1 *Tunnel Jc.*	3 30		3 20		3 47		3 37	
5·5 Porton	9 25	45	8 52	53	10 06	42	9 33	44
11·0 Grateley	15 50	56	15 11	64	16 51	55	16 18	54
17·3 ANDOVER Jc.	20 55	77	20 05	83	22 10	75	21 31	79
22·6 Hurstbourne	25 15	69	24 11	73	26 48	68	25 57	70
24·5 Whitchurch	27 00		25 50	68	28 34	64	27 40	65
28·1 Overton	30 25		—		31 58	62	31 05	60
31·3 Oakley	33 25	61	32 40		34 56	67	34 13	62
			pws	15				
33·4 *Worting Jc.*	—		35 30		36 47	71	36 13	67
35·9 BASINGSTOKE	37 20	76	38 00	71	38 45	83	38 20	
41·5 Hook	41 40	80	42 13		42 50	80	42 40	79
							sigs	10
43·9 Winchfield	43 30	75	—		44 39	81	47 56	
47·2 Fleet	46 05	76	46 24		47 07	80	51 49	58
55·7 Brookwood	53 00		52 45	84	53 37	83	59 35	75
59·4 WOKING	55 45	81	55 21	83	56 18	83	62 26	78
62·0 Byfleet	57 45	81	57 13	83	58 15	81	64 27	81
64·6 Weybridge	59 45	68	59 05	76	60 12	73	66 24	77
70·4 *Hampton C.Jc.*	—	75	63 30		65 03		70 57	73
			pws	30				
71·7 Surbiton	65 40	64	65 22		66 18	63	72 04	69
76·5 Wimbledon	70 00	66	71 07	64	70 54	60	76 10	67
79·8 Clapham Jc.	73 10		74 20		74 40		79 26	37
					sigs			
83·7 WATERLOO	79 00		80 42		83 03		85 53	
Estimated net time (mins)	79		76¾		81¼		80½	

which was to become even a little above that expected twenty-five years later with the greater power then available. Rev. Mortimer clearly got excited about the run – a pleasure not to be denied him – as his notebook's margin is full of notes of so many miles in so many minutes with average speeds in the eighties. This was probably his best run ever and the true enthusiast can

32. Non-standard modification was no. 851 which had
Lemaître exhaust and new cylinders with 8-inch piston
valves but retained the 'piano front' below the smokebox.
Seen here leaving Salisbury on 12 July 1939 with the
12.35 pm to Waterloo.

readily understand (and to some extent share) the elation enjoyed by the cleric.

Last of all are two runs recorded by F. E. Box: no. 865 had the Lemaître exhaust arrangement and the driver was Potter assisted by fireman Whetton. A sedate start to Andover Junction was made but after Basingstoke the dust really did fly and the run had the edge over the epic by this same locomotive on 12 May the previous year. Twelve days later no. 851, the engine with the new, but non-standard, cylinders and Lemaître exhaust, appeared in charge of driver Blaney. There was a faster exit to Andover Junction, a slightly less energetic run up through

33. Driver Payne has time to spare for his photograph to be taken while waiting at Southampton Central for the 'right-away' for the down 'Bournemouth Belle' on 4 July 1939.

69

Oakley and then a bad signal check before Winchfield, which spoiled matters on a fast-running stretch of line. None the less it was an excellent effort and well demonstrated the zenith to which the Lord Nelson class had risen.

What was even more important, however, was that these runs were closely approached daily, as table 12 (a list of other runs recorded by F. E. Box in July 1939) indicates. Mr Bulleid had therefore, by one means or another, not only endowed the class with excellent performance potentiality but had also secured reliability at that high level, an attribute which had hitherto constantly eluded the Operating Department.

Table 12. 'ATLANTIC COAST EXPRESS' JULY 1939

Detail A. WATERLOO – SALISBURY
(Schedule 86 mins)

Loco. no.	Coaches	Tare wt. (tons)	Actual time m.	s.	Net time mins
865	12	388	83	01	82
865	12	387	82	17	80
851	12	385	85	18	82¼
864	12	388	83	48	80¾
858	12	383	83	17	83¼
864	11	355	81	47	81¾
851	12	385	84	15	82
862	12	384	85	39	83¾

Detail B. SALISBURY – WATERLOO
(Schedule 87 mins)

Loco. no.	Coaches	Tare wt. (tons)	Actual time m.	s.	Net time mins
865	13	392	83	03	81½
865	10	289	82	42	78¾
865	12	386	83	27	81½
851	12	387	85	53	80½
864	12	386	82	36	82½
858	11	328	81	08	81¼
851	12	383	81	26	81½
851	10	307	84	36	80

7
Renaissance Stillborn

Despite the impending retirement of driver Fred Payne, who had contributed in no small way to the resurgence of main-line running on the Southern, the stage seemed set in the summer of 1939 for the continuance of the enhanced locomotive performance initiated by the recently appointed Chief Mechanical Engineer.

The Schools class, decked out in the attractive malachite-green livery to match the carriage stock, was performing more than adequately on the Bournemouth route for the second year running and in the process confounding the critics who had prophesied that the water capacity of the tenders would be inadequate for the non-stop London runs. The successful experiment on the Lord Nelson class with the Lemaître exhaust was being extended to the Schools and on the Nelsons themselves the re-designed cylinders were about to become standard equipment so that the next summer would see this hitherto rather unpredictable class become the force it should have been for some years past. All this, coupled with the better-quality fuel now available and the good morale of the footplate staff, really augured well for the immediate future with, of course, the promise of a new passenger design in perhaps a little over a year. In any event, the Nelsons could have a good fling in 1940 before playing second fiddle to the new locomotives.

Alas, the declaration of war on 3 September 1939 blighted these expectations. Apart from the general provisions applying to all locomotive stock, which included, in the case of the Lord Nelson type, the fitting of an anti-glare tarpaulin between locomotive cab and tender front and the blacking-out of the side cab windows, the immediate effect on the class was in the cancellation of the 'Bournemouth Belle', 'Golden Arrow' and continental traffic to Dover. Certainly there were passenger trains carrying personnel to the Channel ports although of a nature not so demanding as the previous services tailored for fare-paying traffic.

For a time there was little change: the country had declared a war which it was unable to prosecute with any vigour because of lack of planning. The locomotive works had not yet been geared up to war production so the general modifications to the Lord Nelson class continued: carrying through the Lemaître exhaust substitution (the programme was completed with nos 857 and 860 in October and December 1939 respectively), the conversion of the tenders to be self-trimming (no. 863 being the last of the sixteen in December 1940) and starting the fitting of the new cylinders of which nos 857 and 860 were the first to have the new standard design.

The evident under-employment of those members of the class on the Eastern Section led to the decision early in 1940 to gather the whole class together on the Western Section at Nine Elms. By February the last resident of the class at Stewarts Lane shed had departed, thus severing a link never again to be re-forged.

When the Allied armies were being swept aside in Northern France and Dunkirk was on the horizon it was evident that the Flaman speed recorder was an item that could well be dispensed with. This equipment was promptly removed and so the class, which had the distinction of being one of the few in the country to be completely equipped with speed-recording apparatus, acquired the added distinction of being one of the few to have had it completely removed.

With the isolation of the country complete, Eastleigh works obviously had more important things to concentrate on – apart from trying to produce a sophisticated 4–6–2 design – and so the general re-equipping of the Lord Nelson class with modified cylinders was dropped in December 1940 when no. 855 acquired the last ones that were to be fitted for many months. By that time, excluding the non-standard examples carried by no. 851, the new cylinders were in service on nos 852, 856, 857, 860, 862 and 865.

The bombing of southern England was becoming more intense and although much of it was of a random nature it was inevitable that railway installations – a legitimate target in any case – would suffer. A certain stoic endurance developed among the populace during the blitz upon London and each person would have his own idea of a good shelter; some would opt for an underground railway station, others for the cupboard under the stairs, while enginemen caught at a locomotive depot would choose a firebox of an engine not in steam. So it was on the night of 16 April 1941 when no. 852, 'Sir Walter Raleigh', suffered a direct hit on the cab while inside Nine Elms shed. A railwayman taking shelter in the firebox was brought out dead. Although damaged, the tender was fairly quickly despatched to Eastleigh works and was accepted for repair on 29 April. The locomotive itself presented a greater problem because the explosion had distorted the rear part and in order to facilitate transport to the works it was necessary to cut the frames off at a point between the two rear axles; the journey was completed on 24 May and the engine was taken into the shops for repair on 16 June, just two months after the incident. New framing had to be welded on and it was not until just over a year after entering works that no. 852 was returned to service – on 20 June 1942 – and then it was in the wartime black livery which had first been applied to no. 859 in May of that year; no. 852 became the second member of the class to be painted in a livery which was to be standard until 1946.

A sporadic return to the fitting of the new design of cylinders came in March 1942 when 'Lord Nelson' itself received these in course of renewal although thereafter the matter was never pursued with any diligence.

As the war progressed and passenger train formations lengthened, the batch of Schools class engines shedded at Bournemouth were finding the task increasingly onerous. Whereas the former non-stop runs or those with a single stop at Southampton could be handled, even if loaded to fourteen bogies, the numerous stops demanded by wartime conditions led to loss of time not only in restarting but also in taking water more frequently because of additional consumption. So in January 1943 nos 850–5 were transferred from Nine Elms to Bournemouth to take over permanently the work which some of the class had previously been doing on a loan basis and six Schools were moved elsewhere.

It was on one of these duties towards the end of the war that no. 854 was employed – the 11.02 am Bournemouth West to Waterloo on 23 April 1945 – when an unusual accident (in some quarters wrongly termed a boiler explosion) occurred. The locomotive ran light from Bournemouth shed to Wimborne in charge of driver Rabbets and fireman Robbins, both Bournemouth men, picked up six empty coaches and proceeded to Bournemouth West and then set out with the 11.02 am departure for Waterloo. At Bournemouth Central the Bournemouth footplatemen were relieved by driver Billett and fireman Perry and with a load of 426 tons (14 coaches) no. 854, which had a month previously been through Eastleigh works and run 6,300 miles since, left on time.

The climb up Hinton Admiral bank was nearly complete when, while travelling at 35 mph near milepost 100, the driver heard a noise he was unable to identify although it seemed that it might be the safety valves blowing off. He then noticed the water dropping in the gauge glass and immediately upon making this observation he was blown on to the tender front and the fireman on to the top of the vacuum reservoirs on the tender. Driver Billett managed to apply the brake from outside the cab and a halt was made 1¼ miles short of New Milton station.

34. Wartime casualty 1: no. 860 in trouble at St Denys with the 3.05 pm ex Bournemouth West on 14 August 1940.

34. National Railway Museum

73

A couple of United States Army medical men and a civilian doctor gave assistance to the fireman who was removed to Boscombe hospital; although making initial progress towards recovery, he had a relapse and succumbed to his injuries on 26 April.

The accident involved damage to the firebox caused by an inrush of steam through a fracture in the crownplate, the boiler being short of water. This inrush of steam also caused the smokebox door to swing open, damaging the left-hand smoke deflector, which became wide of gauge in consequence. The stricken train was rescued by sending no. 345 (a K10 class 4–4–0 on a down goods train) wrong line from New Milton and, as it was considered that this engine would have difficulty in moving 526 tons tender-first up the 1 in 253 grade, no. 1803 (class U 2–6–0) came up to the rear of the train to give assistance. At New Milton no. 345 detached no.

35. Wartime casualty 2: no. 852 'Sir Walter Raleigh' suffered a direct hit in Nine Elms shed on the night of 15/16 April 1941.

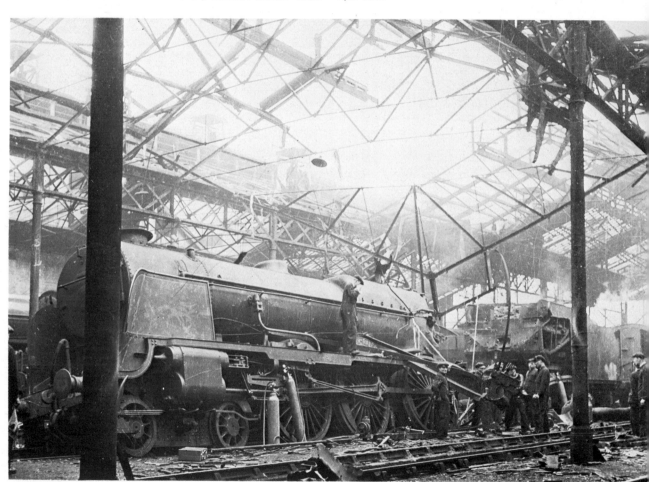

854 and then proceeded to Brockenhurst where no. 1803 ran round and took sole charge, arrival at Waterloo being no more than 78 minutes late.

Somewhat unusually, the Ministry of Transport inquiry preceded the railway company's own investigation. It transpired that the enginemen had thought that the water was above the top of the gauge glass whereas it was below the lower packing nut; one lead plug had partly fused, one entirely and one had started. Mr Bulleid stated that he would not expect that the plugs would behave in a uniform manner. The MOT report placed the responsibility on the driver and fireman in charge at the time of the accident but was critical of the Bournemouth crew who had handed the engine over in such a state. The recommendations which flowed from the inquiry were that a review should be made of the type of plug used which failed to give a warning in time and that gauge glasses should be fitted with backplates having clearly visible stripes to assist with visual indication.

The second point was accepted but the business about the plugs dragged on and had to be raised at a joint committee of the Chief Mechanical Engineers of the railways. Mr Bulleid dictated some typically terse memoranda pointing out that the pellet or drop-type plug was the standard for his 280 lb/sq. in. pressure boilers: eventually, in March 1947, the Ministry of Transport was informed that the Southern Railway was satisfied with pellet fusible plugs and that 'they gave unmistakable warning to engine crews'. There appears to be no indication, however, that any alteration to older engines was intended or required.

A few weeks before this accident the large boiler with round-top firebox (no. 1063) was finally removed from no. 857 and was not used again on the class. With victory in Europe gained and against Japan assured, the desire to return to something approaching normal life was upper-most in everyone's mind and to this end the Southern Railway reverted to repainting its passenger locomotive stock in the malachite-green formerly used, the first one of the Lord Nelson class to be so treated being no. 858 in March 1946. With a large backlog of arrears to be made up the progress could hardly be termed rapid; none the less, the majority of the class were resplendent in this livery before the end of 1947 when the Southern Railway ceased its independent existence.

At the end of the war the class found itself in a very different position to that which it had occupied when hostilities had begun. From being the premier class in the course of rejuvenation for work on the three main routes of the company, it now found itself ousted by the Merchant Navy type on the principal trains and furthermore being rather unexpectedly overwhelmed by the proliferation of the light Pacifics – the West Country/Battle of Britain class. There was to be no return to the Eastern Section but a rather placid existence on less demanding services to and from Waterloo.

When in September 1946 no. 861 starting performing on such trains as the 10.25 am Exeter Central – Waterloo and the 12.50 pm Waterloo – Exeter Central on the section west of Salisbury, some observers were puzzled because the general return of the type to the area was scarcely expected in view of the quantity of Pacific power available. As it happened it was nothing more than one of the whims of Mr Bulleid in comparing coal consumption on identical work of Merchant Navy, Lord Nelson and King Arthur classes, the chosen route being Waterloo–Exeter with a variety of duties. In some cases 14- and 16-coach loads were tackled without much loss of time and overall no. 861 returned a figure of just under 45 lb of coal per mile which was by no means a startling revelation as it appears that it was a fair average for the Lord Nelson class as a

36. No. 857 pictured at Bournemouth West on 18 April 1943 with the large boiler, round top firebox and straight smoke deflectors (compare with Ill. 22).

whole in any case.

Immediately after Christmas 1946, on 27 December, no. 851 was involved in a potentially dangerous accident when approaching Byfleet station on the up through line with the 2.02 pm Bournemouth West–Waterloo train consisting of 12 coaches weighing 394 tons. Speed was in the region of 60 mph when no. 851 suddenly became derailed and ploughed along, destroying over 315 yards of track including a trailing crossover. The engine and coaches veered over to the left, fouling the up local line, but came to a halt only slightly out of the vertical, the leading six-coach set of coaches having buckeye couplings which doubtless contributed to stability. The down through track was dragged out of alignment by the disturbance to the crossover,

while a rail penetrated the tender of no. 851 and one of the tender buffers burst the body of the leading coach. Fortunately no other train was involved and only three passengers were injured, the footplatemen suffering no damage other than, presumably, some shock at finding themselves off the road so suddenly. Poor drainage was the main factor in the waterlogged state of the ballast which caused the faulty cross-alignment of the track; track maintenance arrears was the principal factor leading to the accident in which no. 851 not only was the blameless victim but suffered a fair amount of motion damage.

During the war, in June 1944, no. 859 had been noted working the LMS Royal Train southwards through Wandsworth Common on a rare venture for the class on to the Central Section; 1947, however, was the year when the class really established itself on Royal Train duties on the Western Section for, on 31 January, no. 850

worked from Waterloo to Portsmouth on the occasion of the departure of the King, the Queen and the Princesses for South Africa. The same engine was again used on 12 May on the royal return from South Africa with nos 852 and 854 spare at Fratton and no. 860 standing by at Woking. For the honeymoon journey of Princess Elizabeth and the Duke of Edinburgh from Waterloo to Winchester on 20 November no. 861 was selected having just returned from overhaul at Eastleigh, but in the event no. 857 worked the duty. Although no. 861 did appear at Waterloo complete with smokebox headboard for the benefit of photographers, it was considered that it had not run in sufficiently after overhaul to work the five-coach special. Driver Hawkins had the distinction of driving all three trains.

During the summer the class had started working to and from Oxford with Bournemouth trains via Reading West and, with the close of the year in sight, removal of the two distinctive pressure relief valves mounted on the smokebox, one either side of and behind the chimney, began with nos 861 and 863 in November. The retention of these valves did not warrant the maintenance costs and accordingly they were removed from all classes of locomotives.

At the end of the Southern Railway era the class had been completely fitted with the Lemaître exhaust and high-sided tender. Even so there was still variety in the condition of individual locomotives for, of the sixteen representatives, there were major variations in seven of their number; no. 851 had the non-standard modified cylinders, no. 859 smaller diameter driving wheels, no. 865 the 90-degree crank setting and nos 853, 858, 863 and 864 the original design cylinders. The class was destined never to be uniform even during the long period under nationalisation.

8

Wartime Performance

The outbreak of hostilities had the immediate effect of lessening the demands made upon the class, for the 'Bournemouth Belle' was withdrawn, schedules were eased generally and, with the transfer of those members at Stewarts Lane to the Western Section by early 1940, the whole of the class became concentrated in one area for the first time. Loads were not greatly increased and the additional stops inserted in the timetables meant that the work was not of an unduly exacting nature.

After a while the loads did increase but by then the first batch of the Merchant Navy class 4–6–2 locomotives were at work between Waterloo and Exeter and so the Nelsons were not often called upon to haul the heaviest trains. Nevertheless the period did throw up the occasional run of merit, if not brilliance, and some of these which had the luxury of few or no checks are worth consideration. As in happier pre-war days, the best running usually came on the Salisbury route.

Table 13 has three runs in the down direction, two non-stop between Woking and Salisbury and the other with calls at Basingstoke and Andover Junction. The locomotive in detail A, no. 859 with a 12-coach load, still retained the original type of cylinders. The start was moderate and the climbing to Worting Junction and Grateley was somewhat weak but otherwise the performance was good for wartime. The start (detail B) made by no. 865, which had by this time been fitted with the new cylinders, was rather less promising than that of no. 859, although thereafter, with the heavier load, the work was excellent and on a higher plane throughout. The 36·3 miles from Fleet to Grateley were covered in 32 minutes, which smacked of running in the halcyon summer of 1939, and the delays suffered on the entry to Salisbury were poor reward for some enterprising running. The third run – timed by Mr A. J. Baker as were the other two down runs in the table – has been included as an example of how the class dealt with the heavy semi-fast traffic of the period. The locomotive concerned, no. 854, still retained the old design of cylinders: the work on the first stage was of outstanding quality for the load and outshone the two other runs. Beyond Basingstoke the effort did not greatly diminish and compared very favourably with the non-stop runs.

For the eastbound direction two examples will suffice. The first (detail D), again from the notebook of Mr A. J. Baker, is of no. 857 with a standard boiler (rather than the round-top firebox type it carried for many years) and new cylinders. For the load the climb up to Porton

Table 13. WOKING – SALISBURY

	A 28 July 1941			B 21 June 1941		C 30 Oct. 1942	Detail		D 30 Mar. 1942		E —	
	859			865		854	Loco. no.		857		859	
	12			13		14	Vehicles		13		17	
	370			420		457	Tare load (tons)		420		515	
	390			455		495	Gross load (tons)		455		570	
Mls	m. s.	Speed		m. s.	Speed	m. s.	Speed	Mls	m. s.	Speed	m. s.	Speed
0·0	0 00			0 00		0 00		WOKING	42·1	40 31 sigs		44 22	
3·7	7 00			8 07		7 36		Brookwood	38·4	36 26	77	40 33	
6·7	10 53	47		12 22	45	11 33	51	*Milepost 31*	35·4	34 00	70	38 04	73
12·2	16 39	63		17 58	69	17 07	64	Fleet	29·9	29 38	78	33 43	80
15·5	19 53	58		20 58	64	20 08	64	Winchfield	26·6	27 08	76	31 12	77
17·9	22 15	65		23 07	70	22 16	72	Hook	24·2	25 19	75	29 22	81
23·5	27 38			27 59		28 05		BASINGSTOKE	18·6	21 12	83	25 05	
26·0	30 25	51		30 22	60	6 27	35	*Worting Jc.*	16·1	19 13	71	23 00	
31·3	36 05	62		35 26	67	13 34	61	Overton	10·8	14 17	62	17 22	
34·9	39 36	64		38 28	72	16 45	72	Whitchurch	7·2	10 36	60	13 45	
36·8	41 19	67		40 01	74	18 18	77	Hurstbourne	5·3	8 33	42	10 45	31
42·1	45 59	74		44 12	81	23 26		ANDOVER JC.	17·3	22 36		25 46	
48·5	52 13	48		49 56	52	11 38	48	Grateley	11·0	16 47	54	19 25	
54·0	58 15	68		55 25 sigs	78	17 37 sigs	74	Porton	5·5	9 59	41	11 15	37
58·3	63 01 sigs			60 51 sig. stop		23 16		*Tunnel Jc.* *	1·1	3 48		4 30	
59·4	66 04			70 32		26 06		SALISBURY	0·0	0 00		0 00	
	65½			61½		28+23½+24		Estimated net time (mins)		40		44¼	

*Speed restriction

was reasonable; it was not so energetic as on another occasion when no. 854 with an identical tonnage was through Porton in 9 mins 25 secs at a minimum speed of 43 mph, Grateley in 15 mins 56 secs and, with a maximum of 79 mph, halted in Andover Junction station in 21¾ minutes. Reverting to the effort of no. 857 in March 1942, the net time of 40 minutes for the 42·1 miles from Andover Junction to Woking is notable.

In detail E of this table no. 859 (with the original type of cylinders) had a daunting load of 570 tons gross assigned to it. The smaller driving wheels of this locomotive did not seem to give it any appreciable advantage in climbing up through Porton nor again on the restart from Andover Junction. On the other hand, this same factor did not inhibit some speeding east of Basingstoke either. With such a load one could well appreciate that the crew would be disinclined to thrash the locomotive on the banks; even so, Andover Junction to Woking took no more than 44¼ minutes and the performance was not much removed from work the new Pacific

37. Wartime livery of black for 'Lord Hood' completed by the steel panel in the cabside window and the tarpaulin between cab and tender as an anti-glare measure; note the barrage balloon in the background.

80

engines were doing about the same time on the service, so the old criterion of 500 tons at 55 mph could be successfully attained in the midst of war. It was certainly on a par with 'Atlantic Coast Express' running in 1939 before war broke and demonstrated that the capacity was there to be exploited when the occasion arose.

38. Happier days return with 'Lord Nelson' decked out in malachite-green at the head of the 10.35 am, ex Portsmouth Harbour, Royal Train on 12 May 1947 at the conclusion of the South African tour.

38. LCGB (Ken Nunn Collection)

9
British Railways Era

New Year's Day 1948, which ushered in the nationalisation of the railways in Britain, found six of the Lord Nelsons (nos 856–61) shedded at Nine Elms with the remaining ten members of the class at Bournemouth. Nationalisation, as might reasonably have been expected, was to touch the sixteen locomotives lightly, the changes being mainly confined to livery.

The removal of the pressure relief valves continued as the engines proceeded through works, the last to be dealt with being no. 857 in December 1949. The regional letter prefix applied to locomotive numbers for a short time early in 1948 captured but one Lord Nelson – no. 854 – before giving way to the 30000 addition, for Southern Railway stock, of which the first recipient in the class was no. 856.

Although the rebuilt Royal Scot class of 4–6–0 did figure in the Locomotive Interchange Trials of 1948 other equivalent second-line types, such as the GWR Castle, the LNER Green Arrow and the Southern Lord Nelson, were excluded and an opportunity to contrast the capabilities of these designs was lost. It would have been instructive to see how the Southern men, who drove with such élan on other regions, handled their 4–6–0; exceptional skill would have been needed to match the performance of the Royal Scot in the trials.

Although denied participation in these tests, the class was selected to take part in an exercise to show off proposed liveries of the new ownership to the general public, which involved decking out whole trains in experimental colours and running the ensemble of engine and coaches in regular service. Three representatives of the class were repainted in apple-green with red, cream and grey lining, nos 30861 and 30864 leaving Eastleigh works at the end of May 1948 followed by no. 30856 the next month. These engines were paired with the not unattractive (but not very serviceable) plum and spilt milk liveried coaching stock and performed regularly during the summer on Bournemouth duty 388 which included the 7.20 am from Bournemouth West to Waterloo and 3.30 pm (1.30 pm Saturdays) return. Nos 30856 and 30861, being Nine Elms engines, had to be transferred to Bournemouth shed for the purpose.

For the winter service the stock was switched to the 9.30 am Bournemouth West service from Waterloo and the 2.20 pm return, nos 30856 and 30861 being returned to Nine Elms depot accordingly in the September; the pairing of stock and locomotives became a rather haphazard affair as the novelty of the experiment wore off and doubtless the requirement was adjudged some-

39. Although no. 854 did get an 'S' prefix early in 1948 the first Nelson to be renumbered was no. 30856 which is pictured with Southern Railway style numerals and lettering (the former being shorter in height than the letters). Note also the removal of the snifting valves.

thing of a nuisance by the shed staff particularly concerned. Eventually these two engines lost the livery on visits to Eastleigh in the early months of 1950. While sporting this livery no. 30864 worked a Royal special to and from Southampton on 28 July 1948 for a visit to inspect the liner *Queen Elizabeth*. With the repainting of no. 30862 from black in August 1948 the whole class was in green livery of one type or another but in varying styles of lettering.

Before the Railway Executive finally decided on standard liveries an inspection of various classes and colours was held at Addison Road station on 10 January 1949, for which no. 30853 was specially painted in Southern malachite-green. The result, so far as the Lord Nelsons were concerned, was the selection of the dark

(Brunswick) green with black and orange lining, although it was to be August before the first representative (no. 30863) was so turned out with a large emblem on the sides of the tender.

At the beginning of 1949 the BR power classification for locomotive stock was introduced and the Nelsons found themselves graded 6P, this being amended in May 1951 to 7P when the Merchant Navy class was upgraded. Renumbering of the class was completed in December 1949 with no. 30857 which later sported a small emblem on the tender. February 1951 saw the disappearance of the experimental apple-green livery from the Southern Region when no. 30864 (in company with no. 34065) was given the standard green and by December of that year, with the treatment of no. 30852, the whole class had been dealt with and had the distinction of being the first SR class repainted in BR livery in its entirety.

A curious accident befell no. 30854 on Sunday 20 July 1952 when it was hauling the seven-coach 3.24 pm stopping train from Southampton Central to London. At Eastleigh the train was sent forward on the up local line so that a late-running up boat express from Southampton Docks could overtake it on the up through line before Shawford station, south of which point the local line turned into the through road. The stopping train's fireman was having trouble maintaining steam and because he was devoting all his time to the problem was not able to give driver Greenhough of Nine Elms depot any help in observing signals. On an otherwise clear day the engine was emitting a lot of black smoke which was drifting down and obscuring the driver's vision, as a result of which he mistook the signal for the up through line, which was clear, for that applying to the local line. Too late

the error was realised and, although the brakes were applied, at 3.58 pm the engine overran the signal at danger by 560 yards, derailed itself at about 30 mph in the sand drag and toppled down the 20-foot embankment to come to rest on its side with the tender following, but remaining upright, and the leading bogie of the first coach damaged and derailed.

Neither crew nor passenger casualties were suffered, no obstruction was caused to the adjoining line and the track damage was confined to one rail length in the sand drag. Prompt action in protecting the train was taken by guard Baker, who also stopped the expected boat train, to which passengers from the local train were transferred. Ironically, Shawford was the sole station west of Woking at which the stopping

40. No. 30864 was turned out in experimental apple-green livery with adapted Southern Railway style numerals and lettering to work plum-and-spilt-milk stock.

train was not scheduled to call!

The driver readily admitted that he mistook the signal. It transpired, however, that he had learnt the route ten years previously and had taken a refresher the previous April before working in a link which had this Sunday duty as a completely isolated turn over a route which did not otherwise figure in the trips it undertook. Furthermore, this particular turn came round only twice in a 24-week period for each member of the link. There appears to have been a tacit admission of poor rostering because, by the time of the inquiry into the accident, the duty had already been transferred to a link more familiar with the route.

Some difficulty was encountered in recovering no. 30864 because cranes could not be used. Eventually the engine was jacked upright and then winched up an earth ramp bulldozed specially to get it back to the top level of the embankment. Ten days after the accident the locomotive – the same one that was involved in the New Milton accident some years previously, incidentally – was re-railed, entering Eastleigh works on 7 August to re-emerge after repairs (which were not very extensive) on 6 September. This seems to have been one occasion when a member of the class contributed to its own downfall and that by reason of the old shortcoming of firing difficulties.

41. Nos. 30850 and 30851 present a livery contrast at Eastleigh shed with the former in malachite-green with Gill Sans type lettering and numerals and no. 30851 in BR Brunswick green livery.

42. 'Howard of Effingham' at the foot of the embankment at Shawford after the accident of 20 July 1952.

Apart from slight misfortunes of this nature, or such as when no. 30863 had a heavy encounter with another engine at Eastleigh in 1956, causing it to retire to works for front-end renewal, the class at this time had a placid existence and a good reputation with sheds and works, even if this did not extend to the ranks of the men who had as much to do with the class as any – the firemen. Seldom, if ever, put into store, the class was reliable on summer Saturday and other extras with not too demanding schedules and had an average figure of 81,611 miles between visits to works for general repairs. This compared with 87,424 for the Western Region Castle class, 86,614 for the Eastern Region A4 4-6-2s, 78,987 for the Western Region King class, the

43. In May 1954 no. 30853 leaves Southampton Central with the 2.22 pm stopping train for Bournemouth. This was a part of Eastleigh shed's duty 253 which included standing by at Southampton for the down 'Bournemouth Belle'. Apart from the old-type cylinders the engine and its train is typical of the period.

74,650 of the West Country Pacifics and the 70,495 of the Royal Scot class. Good as these figures are, it may be argued that the Nelsons generally had the lightest duties in proportion to the power available of any of these classes.

As an illustration of the work allocated to the sixteen members of the class the rosters of spring 1954 – when two of the class were re-allocated to Dorchester shed – will serve. There were eight duties in all, of which four were worked by Eastleigh and two each by Bourne-mouth and Dorchester engines. Half of the class was therefore unoccupied although one or two locomotives would be in shops for repair or having a wash-out.

All the work was confined to the Lon-don–Weymouth route with the exception of Eastleigh's duty 251 which incorporated the 10.54 am Waterloo to Salisbury and 4.05 pm return services. The hardest duty was probably Dorchester's 425 which started with a freight to Weymouth and included a non-stop run South-ampton–Waterloo on the 9.20 am ex Weymouth and the 6.30 pm from Waterloo calling only at Southampton before Bournemouth Central.

On Sundays Nine Elms had two duties (one an excursion) for the class, both return workings to Bournemouth; Eastleigh also had a couple, the first involving a Waterloo–Bournemouth–Waterloo–Eastleigh series of trains and the second a return trip to London from South-ampton; while Dorchester had three turns – two of these comprised a return trip to London and the other got as far as Eastleigh before returning on the 1.18 am Monday morning Southampton Terminus to Weymouth semi-fast.

This added up to a weekly revenue-earning mileage of 13,005 for the class of sixteen members (or 813 miles each). There were, naturally, special turns to be worked from time to time, particularly by the Eastleigh-based locomotives. These were mainly on the various ocean liner trains to and from Southampton Docks but did include one or two more exotic turns such as excursions from the Eastleigh area to Exeter, which would give a Lord Nelson a rare chance to pant up Honiton bank. By no means, however, could it be said that the engines were being extended in carrying out their daily routine runs.

This type of duty, varying from time to time in detail but not greatly in scope (through trains to Oxford were in fact included later), occupied

44. W. Philip Conolly

44. The most northerly point that the class reached was Oxford on through trains to and from the Western Region; here, a Castle retires in favour of 'Lord Collingwood' on the Birkenhead–Bournemouth service.

45. Twenty-five years ago, before the days of Concorde, the most luxurious way to cross the Atlantic was by liner. 'Robert Blake' pulls away from the Ocean Liner Terminal at Southampton with passengers from RMS *Queen Mary* comfortably installed in the Pullman cars of 'The Cunarder'.

the class through the 'fifties and was enlivened occasionally, as on 20 January 1956, with a trip on the 13-car up 'Bournemouth Belle' (engine no. 30857); on 4 February following no. 30862 did the honours up from Bournemouth. Between these two runs no. 30859 had established a precedent by working the 4.45 am London Bridge to Brighton (consisting of one passenger coach and a motley collection of fourteen vans), not without some buffeting of its crew.

In March 1957 no. 30857 was the first out-shopping from Eastleigh works to carry the then new BR emblem on its tender. Later that year, on the introduction of the two-hour Bournemouth schedules, a Nelson got the job of work-ing the fast 7.40 pm up from Bournemouth on Saturdays; as it was a light formation and run-ning well out of the period of traffic delays there was no difficulty in keeping the 120-minute schedule.

Ten years of nationalisation passed with little or no alteration to the Nelsons. There had been desultory fitting of modified cylinders (no. 864 in 1948 and no. 858 in 1951) and no. 30852 had acquired, in January 1956, a lower chimney akin to the type which shortly afterwards appeared on the rebuilt Merchant Navy engines; this was the last experiment to improve the steaming of the class. It was all very minor stuff, of course, as might be expected considering that the youngest

46. Some trans-Atlantic travellers could even afford their own trains! Liberace is speeded past Earlsfield by 'Lord Collingwood' on 25 September 1956, towards his waiting fans at Waterloo.

member of the class was nearly 30 years old. There did come something of a crash programme, starting with no. 30862 in June 1958, of modifying the regulator handle and later of modifying the gland and stuffing box thereto, suggesting that some incident had triggered off the alteration. The programme was completed in May 1961 when the second stage of the modification was made on no. 30862. Before this, early in 1958, no. 30853 was the last member of the class to get – very belatedly – the standard modified cylinders; nos 30851 and 30863 never received such cylinders.

The autumn of 1959 saw the whole of the class gathered at Eastleigh and a start being made, with no. 30861, of fitting speedometers, just about 20 years after the Flaman apparatus had been removed. At about the same time the class started to acquire the BR-type automatic warning system (AWS) equipment. No doubt this proved useful when working the 6.22 pm Fridays only Waterloo–Southampton Central–Bournemouth fast train, the boat specials and in fog but otherwise was a nice refinement.

Not all the class got these fittings because the first withdrawal came in May 1961 when the

47. From time to time engineering works would necessitate the closure of the main line and the Nelsons would traverse unusual backwaters – not normally open to the class – such as via Ringwood. In this case 'Lord Duncan' is on the mid-Hants line near Itchen Abbas.

48. The last exhaust modification to be made to a member of the class was the squat cast chimney, like the Pacific type, which was fitted to no. 852. Possibly it improved the locomotive's appearance if not its performance.

31½-year-old no. 30865 was condemned; its tender (no. 1012) was transferred to Schools class no. 30912. After the summer of that year there was a procession to the place of no return. None of the engines suffered the indignity of being sold for cutting up, except that tender no. 1007 from no. 30854, attached finally to Schools no. 30921, did finish its days in the alien area of a

49. Towards the end of the life of the class Eastleigh shed could afford to turn out a Nelson for minor specials such as this 'Mother Goose' excursion; it is interesting that in January 1958, no. 30851 still retained the same non-standard cylinders that it had received in 1939 (see Ill. 32).

Northamptonshire scrapyard. Apart from nos 30852 and 30863, which went to Ashford works for the purpose, scrapping was carried out at Eastleigh. By the time of withdrawal various members of the class had been fitted with manganese axle-box liners to the coupled wheels, water treatment apparatus and various types of injectors, while nos 30861–65 all finished with drop grates.

The summer of 1962 was the last for the class with no. 30861 making a farewell appearance at Exeter Central on 2 September on a railtour train. That was virtually the end. Nos 30861 and 30862 were withdrawn in the October, the last members of the class, each of which had completed about $1\frac{1}{4}$ million miles in service. 'Lord Nelson', which had been withdrawn in August 1962, was put aside for preservation. It went first to Fratton for storage, then to Stratford (Eastern Region) before getting back on to Southern metals at Preston Park (Brighton) in February 1968. There it languished for almost ten years in company with other Southern Railway locomotives earmarked for preservation before going north to Carnforth late in 1977 with hopes of something rather better than the attentions it had received from the pigeons of Sussex. 1980 saw it re-appear as SR no. 850 for 'Rocket 150'.

10

Post-War Performance

With the war over the Nelsons could be said to be approaching the mid-span of their life, assuming a forty-year existence, although in the event (because of accelerated scrapping rates) the halfway mark had already been reached for the majority of members of the class. Despite the proliferation of Pacifics, there was still plenty of work for the sixteen engines. Little of it, however, was to compare with happier days immediately before the war.

There was to be no return to the Eastern Section – save for a couple of lonely scrapping journeys – and even on the Western Section running was confined mainly to Waterloo–Salisbury local trains, Bournemouth–Oxford turns and secondary duties between London and Weymouth. Eventually all the engines gathered at Eastleigh and were used on Southampton boat trains, one-off workings like down Bournemouth Fridays-only trains and suitable local passenger services.

Seldom did any of this work give the opportunity for performance heroics and, even if it did, it was hardly likely to be observed, for there were few recorders who were prepared to spend time logging Nelsons when the Pacifics were better value for money. More often than not such records as were taken of Nelson work were made in the course of compulsory travelling,

which probably gave as good – or bad – a sample of their regular work as could be desired with one or two particular trains.

This appears to have been the case in the majority of the 383 journeys that Mr J. Maidment made behind the class in post-war years. '383 dreary runs', as he describes them, cannot be brushed aside without mention. Most of them were suffered between Woking and Waterloo, especially on the 6.04 am ex Southampton during the period 1957–61 with Eastleigh crews. Standard running with ten coaches (331–360 tons) was 31 minutes net (which was the schedule) and was made 50 per cent of the time. Poor running was experienced on 20 per cent of the runs and better on the remaining 30 per cent, a very good figure, being 29 minutes net. Comparative figures with other classes show the Nelsons up in a poor light, thus disposing of the excuse that these runs were made in times of heavy track occupation when good running was unlikely in any event. Mr Maidment suggests that the principal reason for this was young firemen having difficulty with firing, to judge by the shortage of steam that was often evident.

Fortunately, there were exceptions to the rules. The 6.22 pm Fridays-only ex Waterloo was a job booked for a Nelson, although with a schedule of 89 minutes to Southampton Central

50. 'Lord Nelson' passing Millbrook on an up train from the
New Docks at Southampton.

Table 14. WATERLOO – SOUTHAMPTON CENTRAL

Detail	A		B	
Date	7 July 1961		16 Aug. 1954	
Locomotive no.	30850		30859	
Vehicles	10		12	
Tare load (tons)	336		396	
Gross load (tons)	350		430	
Recorder	Author		M. Hedges	

Mls	Sch.	m.	s.	Speed	Sch.	m.	s.	Speed
0·0 WATERLOO	0	0	00		0	0	00	
			sigs					
3·9 Clapham Junction*	7	8	25	40	7	6	50	52/45
7·2 Wimbledon		12	45	54		10	55	
			sig. stop					
12·0 Surbiton		22	51	35		15	50	64
13·3 Hampton Ct. Junction		24	52	45	18	17	03	68
17·1 Walton-on-Thames		28	45	60		20	32	63/67
						pws		18
19·1 Weybridge		30	42	64/68		24	50	38
24·3 WOKING	29	35	25	64/66	28	30	53	59
28·0 Brookwood		38	51	64		34	44	
31.0 Milepost 31		41	45	62/72		38	00	55
36·5 Fleet		46	39	69		43	22	66
39.8 Winchfield		49	34	65		46	25	63/69
42·2 Hook		51	50	64/67		48	40	65
47·8 BASINGSTOKE*		56	56	62		53	40	72
50·3 Worting Junction*	55	59	25	60	54	56	15	52/50
58·1 Micheldever		66	27	74/82		64	25	70
64·5 Winchester Junction	69	71	16	79	71	69	15	83
66·6 WINCHESTER CITY		72	59		74	72	12	
			sigs					
69·7 Shawford		77	24	52		5	27	55/68
73·6 EASTLEIGH	81	81	12	62	8½	9	05	63/69
			sigs				pws	
77·3 St Denys		86	29			12	53	24
78·2 Northam Junction*	86	88	19		14	15	00	
79·2 SOUTHAMPTON CENTRAL	89	91	32		17	17	50	

| Estimated net time (mins) | 79½ | | 68½+16½ | |

*Speed restriction

it hardly set the blood a-tingling in anticipation unless there were some early delays to ginger up the proceedings. This is precisely what happened on 7 July 1961 (table 14, detail A) when no. 30850 was severely checked crossing over from platform 14 at Waterloo on to the down main and then got stopped at Raynes Park to be switched to the local line, regaining the down main after Surbiton. Consequently it took 25 minutes to pass Hampton Court Junction and that was at reduced speed. By Weybridge running had perked up and Woking was passed 6½ minutes down. Speed did not drop below 60 mph at the summit three miles beyond Brookwood and some fine work was produced right

through to Wallers Ash where the locomotive – then doing 82 mph – was eased. More checks ruined the conclusion of the journey, after being virtually on time at Eastleigh and with a punctual arrival within reach. This run, made in rain, was back to 1938–9 standards although with not such a heavy load as was common then.

The companion log (detail B) was made on the 3.20 pm ex Waterloo in dry conditions with a heavier load and suffered a hampering permanent way check which restricted the start of

51. 'Lord Collingwood', in the final BR livery carried by the class and complete with speedometer and AWS gear, waits to leave Waterloo for Southampton Docks.

51. John Everitt

Table 15. SOUTHAMPTON CENTRAL – BOURNEMOUTH CENTRAL

Detail	A	B	C	D
Date	18 July 1958	4 June 1952	25 Aug. 1955	10 May 1951
Locomotive no.	30860	30855	30855	30862
Vehicles	11	9	13	11
Tare load (tons)	364	304	425	354
Gross load (tons)	386	315	445	365
Recorder	Author	M. Hedges	M. Hedges	M. Hedges

Mls	Sch	m. s.	Speed	Sch.	m. s.	Speed	m. s.	Speed	Sch.	m. s.	Speed
0·0 SOUTHAMPTON CENTRAL	0	0 00		0	0 00		0 00		0	0 00	
2·6 Redbridge*		5 18	46		4 51	50	5 12			5 10	48
6·2 Lyndhurst Rd.		9 39	51		8 59	52	9 30	48		9 15	53
8·8 Beaulieu Rd.		12 33	55		11 41	62/71	12 22	59/64		12 05	58/68
13·6 BROCKENHURST		16 58	65	19	16 23		17 37		20	17 10	
14·5 Lymington Jct.	17	17 57			3 22	31	3 20	28		3 10	26
16·3 Sway		20 00	52		6 15	33	6 42	28		6 30	28
19·3 New Milton		23 05	62	10	9 46		10 44			9 55	56
21·8 Hinton Admiral		25 29	73		4 09	69	4 37	64		12 20	67/70
25·1 Christchurch		28 18	58	8	7 34		8 20		17	15 45	
27·1 Pokesdown		30 23	51	5	5 05		4 57			4 50	26
28·8 BOURNEMOUTH CENTRAL	34	33 04							8	8 25	

*Speed restriction

the climb to milepost 31. Nevertheless, as the figures demonstrate the engine and crew were masters of the situation.

From Southampton to Bournemouth the 6.22 pm Fridays-only London train ran non-stop and detail A in table 15 shows a good effort with no. 30860 on the duty. The intermediate timing of 17 minutes was always optimistic and had probably been arrived at on the basis of half-the-distance-half-the-time which overlooked the nature of the route.

The remaining examples of running in this table are of the usual type of semi-fast work which the class undertook. In detail B no. 30855 was working the 5.30 pm from Waterloo with a seven-minute late departure from Southampton, all of which was recouped by Pokesdown. The same locomotive was hauling the 11.30 am from Waterloo on a hot August day in 1955 (detail C), while the last tabulated run was on the 5.20 pm from Waterloo when very competent work was done. All runs were completely unchecked.

There is no performance beyond Bournemouth worth tabulating so table 16 starts the record of up running. All three runs are of merit and were timed by Mr M. Hedges. The first was the 6.16 pm from Bournemouth West starting

Table 16. BOURNEMOUTH CENTRAL – SOUTHAMPTON CENTRAL

Detail	A			B			C		
Date	18 Sept. 1954			22 May 1953			25 Feb. 1956		
Locomotive no.	30856			30860			30863		
Vehicles	10			11			13		
Tare load (tons)	337			364			431		
Gross load (tons)	360			395			450		
Mls	Sch.	m. s.	Speed	Sch.	m. s.	Speed	Sch.	m. s.	Speed
0·0 BOURNEMOUTH CENTRAL	0	0 00		0	0 00		0	0 00	
1·2 Boscombe		3 17	37		3 23			3 30	32
1·7 Pokesdown		4 07	50		4 15			4 25	43
3·7 Christchurch*		6 05	69		6 10	65		6 35	64
7·0 Hinton Admiral		9 17	61		9 35	55		10 10	50
9·5 New Milton		12 10	51		12 28	48		13 23	42
12·5 Sway		15 13	62		15 17	66		16 38	57
14·3 Lymington Jct.*		17 00	59	18	16 55		18	18 27	
15·2 Brockenhurst*		17 50	68		17 47	70		19 20	72
20·0 Beaulieu Rd.*		21 50	79/65		21 51	74/62		23 31	72/58
22·6 Lyndhurst Rd.		24 13	70/68		24 18	67/65		26 04	
25·5 Totton		26 45	66		27 01	70		28 40	64
26·2 Redbridge*		27 22	63	29½	27 45	46	29	29 22	50
27·9 Millbrook		29 18	50		29 55			31 39	
28·8 SOUTHAMPTON CENTRAL	35	31 20		34½	31 56		34	34 05	

*Speed restriction

ten minutes late from the Central station in wet weather and time was recouped by a disregard (although not an excessive one) of speed restrictions. In detail B no. 30860 was hauling the 5.35 pm from Weymouth and left eight minutes late from Bournemouth. With one extra coach the result was little different from that of no. 30856 in the previous column, except that the Redbridge speed restriction was observed. The third record (detail C) was made on a cold, clear February day and there was no evidence of steam shortage. It was noted that the safety valves lifted after Christchurch and before Beaulieu Road.

Work of a semi-fast nature features in table 17. In detail A no. 30864 was in the BR experimental livery of apple-green with plum and spilt milk painted stock and this coupled with a strong WSW breeze seemed to inspire the crew to get the 7.20 am service from Bournemouth West into every stop before time. Mr Hedges, who has again contributed all the runs in this table, was much surprised and gratified by this above average work and thought it might herald running of a higher order, encouraged by nationalisation and a new livery. His hopes were short-lived however, for when he returned the same day behind the same engine all the vivacity had

99

Table 17. CHRISTCHURCH – SOUTHAMPTON CENTRAL

Detail	A	B	C
Date	21 July 1948	16 Dec. 1951	3 July 1949
Locomotive no.	30864	30865	857
Vehicles	11	11	12
Tare load (tons)	370	370	392
Gross load (tons)	390	405	425

Mls	Sch.	m. s.	Speed	m. s.	Speed	m. s.	Speed
0·0 CHRISTCHURCH	0	0 00		0 00		0 00	
3·3 Hinton Admiral		5 43	44	6 10	45	6 15	41
5·8 NEW MILTON	10	9 05		9 38		10 00	
3·0 Sway		4 34	59	5 41	44	5 30	
4·8 *Lymington Jct.**	7½	6 12	69	7 58		7 15	60
5·7 BROCKENHURST	9	7 50		9 43		9 00	
4·7 Beaulieu Rd.*		6 00		6 46	58	6 45	57
7·4 Lyndhurst Rd.		8 23		9 32	60	9 15	65
10·9 Redbridge*		11 48		13 26	40	12 45	
13·6 SOUTHAMPTON CENTRAL	19	15 29		18 39		17 30	

*Speed restriction

vanished! The second log (detail B) is of the 10 am Sunday ex Weymouth and shows an exact schedule observance overall, the 43 seconds lost to Brockenhurst being countered by gains on the other stages. No. 857 in detail C was also on a Sunday working (6.05 pm ex Bournemouth West) without any lost time incentive.

For the 79-mile journey from Southampton to Waterloo the 91-minute schedules set for the duties to which the Lord Nelsons were assigned provided no great inducement to high power outputs up to Litchfield (Roundwood) and nothing approaching the efforts of the days of 1938–9 is on record. The work performed was generally adequate for the purpose with net times ranging from 84 minutes (very good) to the more usual 87½ minutes.

To conclude there is another of Mr Hedges' records. Again the train is the Sunday 10 am

from Weymouth. The recorder, who joined the train at Bournemouth Central, writes '. . . the start was disgusting – 4½ minutes to Boscombe and schedule exceeded by nearly a third for Christchurch to New Milton, with only 32 mph at Hinton Admiral, dropping to 26 mph on the 1 in 93. Time was even dropped through the Forest, with nothing higher than 60 mph.' All this was with only ten coaches and at Southampton four more vehicles were added. Mr Hedges continues '. . . we got away six late. By Winchester we were eight late and 40 mph was the maximum on the climb to Litchfield.' Basingstoke was left eight minutes late and, after all this dismal and lack-lustre running, matters were suddenly and dramatically transformed, as table 18 records. Excellent work was produced and arrival was not more than 1¾ minutes late, a very substantial load having been whirled along at 70 mph for many a mile.

This is, perhaps, a not entirely unfitting note on which to conclude the record of Lord Nelson performance which for so many years (except for the 1939 zenith) was of a baffling nature, with fleeting bright patches – like the sunshine of an April day.

Table 18. BASINGSTOKE – WATERLOO

Date	23 March 1952
Locomotive no.	30862
Vehicles	14
Tare load (tons)	447
Gross load (tons)	480

Mls	Sch.	m. s.	Speed
0·0 BASINGSTOKE	0	0 00	
5·6 Hook		7 42	63
9·0 Winchfield		9 52	68
11·3 Fleet		12 38	73
14·6 Farnborough		15 20	74
16·8 *Milepost 31*		—	68
19·8 Brookwood		19 42	73
23·5 WOKING	25	22 50	70
26·2 West Byfleet		25 10	69
28·7 Weybridge		27 18	
30·8 Walton-on-Thames		29 15	
34·5 *Hampton Court*			
Junction	37	32 30	61
35·8 Surbiton		33 45	60
38·1 New Malden		36 00	60
40·6 Wimbledon		38 34	58
43·9 Clapham Junction*	49	42 20	34
47·8 WATERLOO	56	49 43	

*Speed restriction

11

Liveries

During the life span of the Nelsons four principal liveries were carried by the whole of the class: the two greens and the wartime black of the Southern Railway and British Railways green. Two experimental greens (the Southern olive and BR apple) were tried on selected engines for short periods.

Works grey marked the first appearance of 'Lord Nelson' (then without nameplates), although the engine was soon adorned with the standard sage- (or Maunsell) green livery adopted by the Southern Railway shortly after grouping. This green was lined out in black and white and the lettering was applied in chrome-yellow. The green extended to the cylinders, the steps and also to the protection guards over the rear bogie wheels – in each instance duly lined out – though this was something of an unnecessary refinement in the last case in view of the oil and dirt that collected on the surfaces. The smokebox, smokebox platform and cab roof were finished in black; the buffer beam was painted red with 'No. 850' applied in the shaded-block style favoured by the LSWR. The nameplates, numberplates on cab sides and the tender back each had a red ground. The power classification letter 'A' was painted on the framing immediately behind the buffer beam each side.

Little variation was made in this arrangement either in the case of 'Lord Nelson' or subsequent members of the class. When smoke deflectors came into use the black of the smokebox was extended to these and at about this time the block lettering on the buffer beam was dropped in favour of the unshaded style which was to become the new standard. Instead of 'No.' the prefix 'E' took its place. When the 'E' prefix was abolished in mid-1931 'No.' returned, although there is a record of no. 851 running without either 'No.' or 'E'. Whereas the old-style abbreviation for number consisted of a capital 'N' followed by a small 'o' set high and a line beneath it, the new style set the line higher and placed a stop beneath the line. With the dropping of the 'E' prefix new numberplates were cast for the cab sides and those on the rear of the tender were dispensed with in favour of painted numerals.

No other amendment was made until 1938 when nos 855 and 862 appeared with the cylinders lined out in a panel instead of vertical lining on the front and back edges. Nos 852 and 855 were the only members of the class to acquire high-sided tenders in the old livery while no. 863 was the sole locomotive to carry a large stove pipe chimney in that same livery. The combination of sage-green and a standard large-diameter chimney never occurred.

Although some of the Schools class were being turned out in 1938 in malachite-green it was olive-green that marked the first change for the Nelsons. In November 1938 some of the engines selected for the exhaust experiments were equipped with stove pipe chimneys and turned out in olive- (or Dover) green lined out in cream and dark green with plain black cylinders; these were nos 855, 856, 861 and 863. The smoke

deflectors remained black but the numberplates were removed and new-style numbers (9 inches high and gilt with a black shadow) were painted on the cab sides. The tenders bore the one word 'SOUTHERN' (also 9 inches high) on each side, and this was in line with the cab numerals on nos 855 and 861 (which had high-sided tenders) but at a lower level on nos 856 and 863 which retained the unmodified tenders. The numerals on the front buffer beam were larger than used hitherto and the abbreviation 'No.' was dropped.

52. For a short time in the early 'thirties the 'E' prefix to the number appeared on the front buffer beam as this shot of no. E852 on a boat train clearly shows.

53. When the 'E' prefix to the number was dropped, the numberplate on the rear of the tender (see Ill. 9) was removed and the number painted on, as in the case of no. 857 here.

The remaining locomotive engaged in the exhaust experiments – no. 864 – was turned out in the old sage-green but in the same general style for lettering and the like. As it had a modified tender the numbers and lettering lined through.

Further engines were turned out in the olive-green – Nos 852, 854, 858 and 859 – with variations in lining and for nos. 852, 858 and 859 the smoke deflectors were finished in green and lined out. No. 854 was the sole example of an engine with the original type of chimney being decked out in a new livery.

This olive-green trial then gave way in favour of the malachite-green, the first to be treated being no. 853 on receiving the standard large-diameter chimney. The cylinders remained black but the smoke deflectors were lined out in a green panel, that part of the deflector coming below the top edge of the cylinders being painted black. At first the lining was yellow and dark green, but black soon replaced the dark green. The low lettering on the old tenders continued until all were converted to the new standard. The large numerals on the front buffer beam did persist in some cases (eg. nos 851 and 853) but

54. Probably the reason why drivers always referred to engines by number was because from the ground they could not see the name! Note the half-height 'T' set high in the abbreviation in 'Lord St Vincent'. 'Howard of Effingham' was the other odd nameplate having the middle word in half-height capitals.

others, such as nos 850 and 854, continued with the type that had been standard for many years.

Malachite-green, due to the pressures of war, eventually had to be replaced by something plainer and in May 1942 no. 859 came out from Eastleigh works with the answer – plain black relieved only by malachite-green shaded (or Sunshine) lettering and numerals. The style of numerals used on the cab sides was also used (6 inches high) for the front buffer beam.

Four years of this sombre livery passed before a reversion was made to malachite-green in March 1946 when no. 858 reappeared in that colour. A link with the black was seen in the buffer beam numerals which remained the same

55. Livery variation in 1939: no. 859 has its smoke deflectors painted entirely in green rather than in panels, and because it still carries an unmodified tender the lettering on it does not line up with the numerals on the cabside.

as on the cab sides, while the steps and bogie covers did not regain the green of pre-war days.

Nationalisation was, of course, to bring a change. Not unnaturally the first alterations were adaptations of existing livery with the title 'BRITISH RAILWAYS' appearing on the tenders in the same style as 'SOUTHERN' had previously. Only one Lord Nelson (no. 854) got an 'S' prefix and this was applied in front of the number on the cab sides but about half the size of the numerals. When the 30000 addition to the class numbers was made this also was done in the old Southern style. With the introduction of cast smokebox numberplates the buffer beams became blank and, when British Railways adopted Gill Sans lettering as standard, cab numerals and tender lettering followed that fashion. After a time the tender sides were left blank.

The 'Show-the-public' apple-green experiment of the summer of 1948 caught up three of the class (nos 30856, 30861 and 30864). The lining in this scheme was red, cream and grey and areas painted green were the same as for the malachite-green except that the smoke deflectors reverted to black and the wheels took that colour also; two other noticeable alterations were the moving of the power classification 'A' to below the cabside numerals, and the lining out of the tender which, instead of strictly following the perimeter, cut across horizontally on the break line where the side sheet canted in. Tender lettering was in Gill Sans but the cab numerals were wartime Sunshine type modified to save expense; these soon gave way to Gill Sans.

Blue livery was chosen by BR for the first-rank express locomotives. Such an exotic colour was not for the Nelsons, however, which had to be content with Brunswick green lined with black and orange. The first application of this was to no. 30863 in August 1949 when it was seen that it perpetuated the variations made with the apple-green save that the numerals were in Gill Sans, the lion-and-wheel emblem adorned the tender sides, the lining to the cab was confined to a panel below the window, and the black cylinders had orange vertical lines at front and rear edges. Apart from the alteration in the type of emblem on the tender (the first Nelson to have this was no. 30857 in March 1957) and the addition of the BR power classification on the cab side, this livery did duty for the remaining years of the class.

12

Assessment

What, then, should be the verdict on the Lord Nelsons? It can hardly be recorded that the class was an unequivocal success any more than it was a complete failure. Curiously it is difficult to single out even one or two really great performances as one can with the King Arthurs, the Schools or the Bulleid Pacifics.

Although the ability to attain a speed of 100 mph is not the sole yardstick of a locomotive's capabilities, it is a popular one and therefore some reference to it should be made in passing. There appears to have survived no checkable record of a Lord Nelson reaching this figure, although Mr S. C. Townroe has indicated to the author that speeds of over 100 mph were recorded between Dorchester and Wareham, at the time the Flaman recorders were fitted on the engines in 1938–9, with light trains – about 135 tons – on falling grades. The evidence in the form of the recording rolls is lacking because of the demands of the wartime wastepaper drive.

Another report was of no. 852 attaining 100 mph approaching Winchester on a down test train composed of ten Pullman cars on a 100-minute schedule from Waterloo to Bournemouth Central. One minute was dropped on the 49-minute booking to Worting Junction, which loss was recouped by Winches-

ter and the run was made in a shade under the 100 minutes laid down. So far as can be gathered this run was made in January or February of 1938 and may have been in connection with the single blastpipe trials. This effort was phenomenal for the class and it is a thousand pities that nothing more of it is on record.

About a year later no. 864, in the course of experiments with the multiple-jet exhaust, is reported to have passed milepost 31, hauling ten bogies, at 79 mph after being checked for signals to 30 mph at Woking. This, of course, has nothing to do with 100 mph running but is placed on record as the third of the feats of the class which could really rank as outstanding but of which data is so slight. Each of these three fall into the 1938–9 period which an earlier chapter has referred to as the zenith for the class.

Most things in life are children of their time and as far as the Lord Nelsons were concerned, time played a disproportionate part in shaping the career of the type, a consideration of which throws up certain interesting points.

The first phase really extends from 1926, when 'Lord Nelson' emerged from Eastleigh, until April 1927, when the final test run with the prototype was made. The engine was very much under official eyes and at first had an unreal existence with one driver travelling with it

56. Livery variation in BR days: no. 30857 displays a small emblem on the tender.

wherever it went on none-too-taxing trial runs. This evident restraint was perhaps well justified in the very wet summer of 1927 which was blamed for a series of derailments culminating in the accident at Bearsted on 20 August and the disaster at Sevenoaks a few days later. On the Great Western the down 'Cornish Riviera Express' escaped serious trouble by a hair's breadth only two weeks before the Sevenoaks accident when the bogie of no. 6002 became derailed near Midgham and hit the metalwork of a girder overbridge without causing further damage; derailments on the GWR also occurred at Kidderminster and Menheniot and in most of these cases the trouble could be traced to poorly drained track. The Bearsted and Sevenoaks accidents were, coincidentally, on the very

routes that 'Lord Nelson' was working and one wonders whether the class would ever have grown had it been no. E850 that had been involved instead of River class tank engines.

Rough riding had already been noted by Holcroft in December 1926 near Woking as a result of which he had recommended that the helical springs to the bogie wheels be replaced by those of the laminated type. Add to this Gresley's comment on the poor condition of the Southern Railway's main line track when he was conducting tests in October 1927 following the Sevenoaks derailment and it will be readily seen that running tended to become restrained on the SR. Furthermore, the centre of gravity of 'Lord Nelson' was fairly high at 5 ft 7½ ins.

This led into phase 2 which lasted a long time

while the main line track was being brought up to a satisfactory state; nor did the derailment and re-railment at Kent House in January 1930 help matters. Enginemen could hardly be blamed for

being loath to give engines their head in view of the possibility of coming off the road.

Phase 3 was entered about 1935 or 1936 when track improvements had taken place. At the same time the class underwent – some might say suffered – an alteration in the lead to the valves from $\frac{1}{4}$ in. to $\frac{3}{16}$ in. to fall into line with a modification made to overcome a certain diffi-

57. 'Lord Nelson' reviews some of the Warship fleet at Paddington on 24 June 1962 before setting out on a railtour train.

culty in the Schools class. This amendment was made with the benefit of standardisation in mind rather than being born out of necessity in the case of the Nelsons.

Bulleid's advent signalled phase 4, which lasted no more than a couple of years. The lead to the valves was again amended, coal quality was improved, encouragement to enginemen was given and the exhaust and other modifications which were carried out during the period all combined to help in better performance – in fact the best performance that the class was to produce.

War heralded phase 5 and a restoration of $\frac{1}{4}$-in. lead to the valves: the final phase was the period covered by nationalisation which was characterised by the class operating duties of a secondary nature with limited opportunities to display any prowess.

To a large extent it could be said that the years which gave greatest opportunity to the class were 1935 to 1939. The latter part of these five years was rewarding with work on the Bournemouth line providing EDHP figures of 1450

58. The last Nelson from Exeter was no. 30861 'Lord Anson' on 2 September 1962 on a railtour working; the following month the engine was withdrawn and the class – apart from the preserved no. 30850 – had disappeared before the year's end.

(1750 IHP) on the climb up through Winchester and the chalk to Litchfield summit, quite the best figures to be produced by the class. The earlier part of this period produced little, possibly because of the first valve lead alteration.

Two particular charges have been made against the class, namely that the front end and cylinder arrangements were inadequate, and that steaming was fitful. The first of these suggestions overlooks the facts that the same design – except for three cylinders instead of four – was found on the Schools class which never came in for criticism on this score, and also that the best work in 1938–9 was with the original arrangement. There would therefore appear to be little substance in this charge.

Fitful or erratic steaming seems always to have been something of a problem, except possibly in the halcyon 1939 summer. The part-flat/part-sloping grate with the brick arch low at the point where the slope began had always been

59. The last journey of no. 30863 'Lord Rodney' was with an engineers' train from Hither Green to Tonbridge (seen here passing Knockholt) on 3 February 1962, en route to Ashford works for scrapping. This engine retained the original design of cylinders throughout its life.

60. Showing signs of having been liberally anointed by the pigeons of Brighton, 'Lord Nelson' is hauled through Bedford on 19 November 1977 en route, eventually, for Carnforth. Its boiler is no. 821 and the tender no. 1003.

60. David Fatwell

59. S. C. Nash

the dread of some firemen (which they readily confirm), even in BR days. The firebox being 18 inches longer than a King Arthur type demanded a further throw on the part of the fireman to keep coal to the front. The penalty for not keeping the front of the firebox well fed was a thin fire and a lot of air being pulled in, and this could be accentuated by a pile-up of coal not reaching the front. Such a combination brought in its wake the inevitable fall in steam pressure which was difficult to remedy while in motion.

Some firemen mastered the art of firing the class, while others were less successful, which probably accounted for reports of the same engine returning vastly different performances

within a matter of days. Taking all the evidence into account it would seem fair to say that there were few firemen that would rue their ill-luck in missing an opportunity to fire a Nelson either before or after the war. The chance in 1947 to include some or all of the class in the oil fuel scheme, to see if the esteem in which firemen held the type could be improved, went by ungrasped.

If the fireman did not do well with a particular type of engine then it followed that the driver would share the dislike because he did not have at his disposal the sole commodity the fireman was there to provide – steam. Attention had to be given to the inside cylinders and motion

61. Restoration begins on 'Lord Nelson' at Carnforth in September 1979 as the boiler is lifted.

which was the driver's responsibility and this explains an answer to a query made of a driver as to his comment on the type which came in the form, 'They were four-cylinder engines . . .'. Apart from this no especial dislikes were apparent. Reliability was good in later years and maintenance costs were not heavy.

There is no doubt that the class in its first decade fell short of expectations; its performance did not measure up to its potential and it lacked the intangible essential for flair. The improvements instigated by Bulleid enabled performance to match more surely what was expected originally. That this should fall away again in later years was regrettable but not entirely to be unexpected.

One point still does remain indisputable. 'Lord Nelson' was the progenitor of Maunsell's greatest design and indeed the finest 4-4-0 locomotive ever built – the Schools class. That is the proper niche in history for 'Lord Nelson'.

Appendix
Construction, Modification and Withdrawal Dates

No.	850	851	852	853	854	855
Built	8/26	6/28	7/28C	9/28D	10/28	11/28
Tender modified	6/39	6/39	11/37	10/40	2/39	8/38
Flaman recorder	9/38	6/39	4/39	4/39	2/39	8/38
Olive- (Dover) green livery	–	–	4/39	–	2/39	11/38H
Lemaître exhaust	6/39	6/39	4/39	4/39	6/39	9/39L
Malachite-green livery	6/39	6/39	–	4/39	6/39	9/39
Modified cylinders	3/42	6/39N	3/40	2/58	11/46	12/40
Black livery	4/44	1/44	6/42	2/43	12/43	4/43
Malachite-green livery	11/46	11/46	3/47	11/48	11/46	5/47
Snifting valves removed	11/48	1/49	3/49	11/48	6/49	2/49
BR renumbering	11/48	1/49	3/49	11/48	6/49B	2/49
BR green livery	1/51	10/50	12/51	7/50	10/51	9/50
AWS gear	12/60	9/60	8/60	4/60	10/59	6/60
Speedometer	12/60	9/60	8/60	4/60	–	6/60
Withdrawn	8/62	12/61	2/62	3/62	9/61T	9/61
Cut up	P	5/62	3/62	4/62	9/61	2/62

Notes: A – Apple-green livery acquired (see page 107)
        B – 'S' prefix 3/48
        C – Six-wheel tender until 11/29 and Urie-type tender until 6/32
        D – Six-wheel tender until 1/30 and Urie-type tender until 2/32
        E – Urie-type tender until 6/32
        F – Urie-type tender until 5/31 and fitted with longer boiler (no. 860)
        H – Fitted with large-diameter chimney and involved in exhaust experiments
        K – Kylchap-type exhaust and double chimney fitted (no. 862 in 8/34 and no. 865 in 3/38)

856	857	858	859	860	861	862	863	864	865
12/28	12/28R	2/29E	3/29E	4/29F	9/29	10/29K	10/29	11/29	11/29K
7/40	10/39	5/40	1/40	12/39	11/38	4/40	12/40	11/38	9/40
11/38	10/38	5/39	11/38	12/39	11/38	10/38	11/38	11/38H	6/39
11/38H	–	5/39	5/39	–	11/38H	–	11/38	–	–
8/39L	10/39	5/39	5/39	12/39	10/39L	5/39	6/39M	6/39L	6/39
8/39	10/39	5/40	1/40	12/39	10/39	5/39	6/39	6/39	6/39
7/40	10/39	1/51	12/46	12/39	8/43	4/40	–	5/48	9/40
9/42	1/43	9/42	5/42	10/42	8/43	7/43	11/42	6/43	5/43
6/46	6/46	3/46	12/46	1/47	11/47	8/48	9/46	2/47	6/46
4/48	12/49	1/48	1/48	11/48	11/47	8/48	11/47	5/48	8/48
4/48A	12/49	6/48	2/49	11/48	5/48A	8/48	8/49	1/48A	8/48
4/50	12/49	1/51	3/51	10/50	3/50	2/51	8/49	4/51	11/49
9/60	7/60	10/59	9/59	12/60	12/59	5/61	10/59	10/59	–
9/60	7/60	–	–	12/60	12/59	5/61	–	–	–
9/62	9/62	8/61	12/61	8/62	10/62	10/62	2/62	1/62	5/61T
11/62	10/62	11/61	12/61	8/62	11/62	10/62	2/62	3/62	8/61

L – Fitted with standard Lemaître exhaust and large-diameter chimney
M – Fitted with large-diameter chimney and involved in exhaust experiments 6/38
N – Non-standard modified cylinders
P – Preserved
R – Non-Belpaire boiler (no. 1063) fitted from 1/37 to 9/41 and from 1/43 to 2/45
T – Tender 1007 from no. 30854 transferred to no. 30921 and tender 1012 from no. 30865 to no. 30912

References are to month and year. Thus 8/26 indicates August 1926.

Index

120